CYRIL OF ALEXANDRIA

CHRISTOLOGICAL DIALOGUE ON THE INCARNATION OF THE ONLY-BEGOTTEN

Foreword by
Rev. Fr. Michel Najim, Ph.D.

Translation and Introduction
Emmanuel Gergis, Ph.D.

Edited by
Ramez Mikhail, Ph.D.

AGORA
UNIVERSITY
PRESS

CYRIL OF ALEXANDRIA : CHRISTOLOGICAL DIALOGUE ON THE
INCARNATION OF THE ONLY-BEGOTTEN

Copyright © 2020 by Agora University Press

All rights reserved. Printed in the United States of America. No part of this book may be used or reproduced in any manner whatsoever without written permission except in the case of brief quotations embodied in critical articles or reviews.

Cover photos by Aidan McRae Thomson

For information contact: aupress@aui.ac
Agora University Press: aupress.org

ISBN : 978-1-950831-05-0

Third Edition : June 2020

HIS HOLINESS POPE TAWADROS II
118th Pope and Patriarch of the great city of Alexandria and the See of St. Mark.

HIS HOLINESS PATRIARCH IGNATIUS APHREM II
Patriarch of Antioch and All the East.

PRINTED IN THE UNITED STATES OF AMERICA

DEDICATION

THIS BOOK IS DEDICATED TO

GOD INCARNATE

SAINT CYRIL OF ALEXANDRIA,
THE PILLAR OF ORTHODOX FAITH

MY PARENTS MICHAEL AND ALICE

MY WIFE MONICA, AND CHILDREN LUKE AND HELENA

EVERY HUMAN BEING
WHO IS SEEKING THE INCARNATE LOGOS

FOREWORD

This important project originated at the Antiochian House of Studies in Pennsylvania, as Emmanuel Gergis, a brilliant student, was planning to work on his master's thesis topic for the Master of Arts degree in Applied Orthodox Theology through the University of Balamand. Among the many subjects that students chose, Emmanuel came up with the idea of translating and writing an introduction to the dialogue between Saint Cyril of Alexandria and Hermias the priest on the "Incarnation of the Only-Begotten Son".

Seeing the luminosity of Emmanuel, I agreed to be his first reader, although I knew that his Greek language was then not sufficient to deal with Cyril's complex and archaic Greek. With great determination, Emmanuel was able to improve his Greek, and before long became competent enough (with the help of the French language) to translate this important dialogue into English. Translating such an intricate text is not a painless task, but thanks to the effort of Emmanuel, Cyril's text is available for the first time to the English-speaking readers.

Needless to say, the numerous characteristics of saint Cyril's Christology, as manifest in this book, may be used as guidelines for the burning issues of modern Christianity's battle with post-modernism. As a conclusion from the points listed in Emmanuel's introduction, we may say that saint Cyril's matrix can be used as a common standard for both Chalcedonian and non-Chalcedonian traditions. Cyril's Christology would be the foundation to reach complete Christological conformity between these two families.

I am hoping that this labor, which has been completed with love and steadfast determination, will manifest the shared Christology between these two families. Being oriented towards the Christological truth manifested in the Holy Scriptures, an essential of the Tradition of faith, having come down to us from the Holy Apostles themselves, this dialogue will be an exemplary text to deepen our understanding of the Christological teaching of the church.

I know how necessary it is that we should be fed by the Christological truth of saint Cyril. Certainly, the benefit of reading this text must come to the soul by way of contemplation of such great mystery of the incarnation. Reading Saint Cyril's text is a spiritual treasure for the reader.

I express my gratitude to Emmanuel, and my highest appreciation for his diligent academic dedication.

V. Rev. Michel Najim, Ph.D.
President of the Antiochian House of Studies

ACKNOWLEDGMENTS

It is almost trite to say, no work is produced in an individual vacuum, as the spirit of our Orthodox Church is the communal spirit of sharing, one can even say that God created the whole world for His incarnation, and He was incarnate in order to share with humanity, as expressed by St. Cyril of Alexandria himself in the Coptic Orthodox rite of midnight praises: "He took what is ours, and gave us what is His." So, first and foremost, I would like to thank my Lord Jesus Christ for giving me the strength and determination it took to complete this project.

I am so grateful for the great amount of support that His Grace Bishop Serapion has given me to bring this book to fruition. His Grace's enthusiastic interest in the writings of St. Cyril of Alexandria has been a constant support and a great source of inspiration.

It was Rev. Fr. John Paul Abdelsayed who first encouraged me to translate this work as a part of my Master's program in Applied Orthodox Theology at the University of Balamand. I acknowledge with gratitude his selection of this text. My gratitude also goes to V. Rev. Fr. Michel Najim, my advisor and mentor who directed this project. His spirituality, erudite insight and academic experience have been a tremendous aid to me throughout this task. I also acknowledge Rev. Fr. David Hester who reviewed this thesis as my second reader.

The success of this book is also attributed to the invaluable help of Ramez Mikhail, who reviewed the translation from the original Greek, and spent endless nights editing and refining the translation. I am greatly indebted to his assistance and vigilance. His perseverance has been a motivation to me in stressful times.

Last, but by no means least, my heartiest thanks go to my wife Monica Ghattas. It is because of her lengthy patience and support that I could accomplish this endeavor. Thank you Monica, you are a gem.

CONTENTS

DEDICATION III

FOREWORD IV

ACKNOWLEDGMENTS VI

INTRODUCTION 1

THE TRANSLATION 25

BIBLIOGRAPHY 94

BIBLICAL CITATIONS 96

ABOUT THE TRANSLATOR 103

Introduction

The work at hand is a dialogue between Saint Cyril of Alexandria and Hermias the Priest[1] on the "Incarnation of the Only-Begotten Son". As with many Cyrillian works, the Dialogue on the Incarnation is a matter of scholarly dispute. Complicating this dispute is the striking similarity between the Dialogue and Cyril's *Oratio ad Theodosium* which is believed to be published in the spring of 430 A.D.[2] Those scholars who believe that the *Oratio* was published first, and the Dialogue is an edited version of the former, date the Dialogue in or after the

---

[1] Hermias is the character that Saint Cyril is dialoguing with in this work. Scholars seem to differ on his real identity as historical resources lack to have any real information about him. Hermias is also mentioned in Περί Αγίας τε και Ομοουσίου Τριάδος (PG 75, 600A-661D). In the dialogue on the Trinity, he is portrayed as an older man who cannot leave his house because of his ailments. Scholars also seem to hesitate on confirming that Hermias in the dialogue on the Trinity is the same character mentioned in this work, or even the one mentioned in Ὅτι εἷς ὁ Χριστός (PG 75, 1253-1361). Furthermore, other scholarship suggests that he is a fictitious character that was invented by Saint Cyril for the sole purpose of the dialogues, especially that the name Hermias was fairly popular in Greek philosophical circles. Finally, G. M. Durand completely disqualifies the theory that the Hermias mentioned in this dialogue is the same as Hermias the philosopher who wrote Διασυρμός των έξω Φιλοσόφων as mentioned in Cyrille, *Deux dialogues christologiques* (Paris: Éd. du Cerf, 1964), 188–189.

[2] Ibid., 43.

spring of 430 A.D.[3] Later scholars, who found the language of the Dialogue less cautious, have argued that the Dialogue was published at an earlier date.[4] De Durand has argued that St. Cyril had changed those terms which could be interpreted or wrongly adopted by Nestorian parties in the *Oratio*.

Thus, the Dialogue could date to 428 A.D. or even earlier.[5] This most probably explains the reason why St. Cyril does not mention Nestorious by name, or the form of dialogue. These latter scholars have also argued that it was attached as an appendix to the Dialogues on the Trinity. It is interesting to note, that most of St. Cyril's theological works before 428 were written in dialogue form— e.g. *De Adoratione, Dialogues on the Trinity, Dialogue on the Incarnation, That Christ is One*. However, after the Nestorian Controversy, this format was rarely used by the Patriarch.

In this dialogue, St. Cyril strongly refutes four erroneous doctrines. He fundamentally attacks from the beginning the notion of Christological dualism, persistently confessing Alexandrian

---

[3] Hans van Loon, *The Dyophysite Christology of Cyril of Alexandria* (Leiden; Boston: Brill, 2009), 259, http://public.eblib.com/EBLPublic/PublicView.do?ptiID=489511.

[4] This argument was primarily made by A. Dorner, as mentioned in I. A Dorner and William Lindsay Alexander, *History of the Development of the Doctrine of the Person of Christ*. (Edinburgh: T. & T. Clark; [etc.], 1868), 55.

[5] Some Scholars like Fr. George Dragas believe that this text was actually written in 432 A.D., but there is no supporting data for this claim. See Cyril and George Dion Dragas, *Against Those Who Are Unwilling to Confess That the Holy Virgin Is Theotokos* (Rollinsford, NH: Orthodox Research Institute, 2004), xvii.

Christology.

1. **Docetism:**

St. Cyril begins with Docetism because he believed that it was, in chronological order, the most ancient heresy that had threatened the faith in Christ. The very use of the generic name "Docetism", which is a trend rather than a specific sect, makes it difficult to believe that our saint was addressing the Manichean view.

His defense against Docetism has us suppose that he recognizes the existence of such gnostic belief among his contemporaries, people willing to belittle everything that is flesh, and thus volatilizing the Incarnation: the notion that declares that the virginal conception cannot be imagined as the Savior disdained a carnal flesh. But the refutation of this heresy, conducted early enough in the text, is not really only a list of verses, or a large reinforcement of Biblical quotations, but rather major explanations of "the mystery of godliness"[6], showing that these events are devoid of any sense if Christ is not a real flesh.

This, says St. Cyril, is the truth. The Only Begotten Son had no other purpose in becoming man, but to reveal Himself to the

---

[6] 1 Timothy 3:16.

beings of the earth. Now to summarize this concept of the incarnation to Hermias, St. Cyril uses many Bible verses to emphasize that God Himself came in the flesh. He knows that the Word will not really be Emmanuel – God with us – if He cannot be seen, and assumes a tangible flesh. Moreover, Christ cannot simply be a shadow or an apparition; He must be a Divine force working from within our race to lift us up to be partakers of the true life.

2. Metamorphosis of the Incarnation:

The second heresy challenged by St. Cyril may be even more equivocal than that of Docetism. We cannot, it seems, track the heresy to any of the heretics whose names have come down to us, but we find some traces of this heresy around the years 350-380 through a series of articles condemning those who see the transformation of flesh as a result of the incarnation of the Word of God. There are several clues pointing to Asia Minor as the place of development of this idea.

However, there is at least one written evidence that its circulation was wider and also could not escape St. Cyril's attention. It's the Letter of St. Athanasius to Epictetus[7], which devotes a few lines to refute the allegation that "the Word was transformed into flesh, bones, and a skeleton as a whole, in exchange for His own

---

[7] Philip Schaff, *NPNF2-04. Athanasius: Select Works and Letters* (CCEL, n.d.), 570–574.

nature." It does not appear, however, that St. Cyril has taken full account of the work of his predecessor to fight this heresy, where the Defender of Nicaea used John 1:14 to indicate the impossibility of a transformation in the Divine nature to the flesh or the curse, but (an assumption of humanity by the Word).

Nevertheless, St. Cyril's argument here rests on a more metaphysical foundation, so to speak, namely the strong opposition that there is always a difference between God and creatures, immutability and change. Our author has no difficulty supporting this principle with Biblical quotations, and obviously depending on Phil. 2:5-11 to clarify his notion of κένωσις.

3. **Marcellus and Photinus:**

St. Cyril then reported a heresy that corresponds roughly to the ideas generally attributed to the two heretics Marcellus and Photinus. Marcellus assumes a gradual expansion of the "Monad" where God the Son (and the Holy Spirit) would emerge from the one God, which, in his teachings, was due to the needs of their economy, as separate entities. Photinus on the other hand professes a distinction between the Word and the Son, one permanent, without a personality attribute, and the other does not begin to exist until only at the time of the incarnation.[8]

The Patriarch of Alexandria uses strong arguments with detailed Biblical quotations to support the true Orthodox doctrine. Rooted in this tradition, our doctor places a lot of confidence in the notion of the image, judging it as proper to eloquently describe the nature of the Son and to establish His eternity. He clarified to his interlocutor that "images are like their Archetype". St. Cyril here exerts a lot of effort to rehabilitate the idea of the Word, to show that He is more than a simple word merely uttered.

4.   **Christological Dualism:**

This heretical doctrine is discussed at the beginning of our dialogue. The discussion on dualism is justified quite well from a simply chronological point of view, but it is nonetheless undeniable that St. Cyril has reserved this discussion for the end to be at liberty to make his exposition as long as he wants. Through this strategy, he manages to pose the problem in terms most favorable to him.

As Cyril explores dualism, Hermias does a little more than "repeating the word who?" Who is Jesus Christ, was He given birth by St. Mary? Did He speak to the Samaritan woman? How does He deserve our worship? How can He therefore contain two elements as

---

[8] Aloys Grillmeier, *Christ in Christian Tradition* (Westminster John Knox Press, 1996), 274–296.

incompatible as the divinity and humanity, without each of them suffering permanent harm, one absorbed in an excess of glory, while the other weakens compromised in corruption?

While He strives to prove that his opponents confess two Christs and two sons, St. Cyril argues in a way that is quite significant. For him, it is plausible to say: Jesus of Nazareth is eternal, "or" the Word was born of Mary". In various forms, St. Cyril responded: yes, the one in whom we have been baptized is one and the same Word of God.

Manuscripts and Sources

In preparation for this translation, two sources were primarily used. Saint Cyril of Alexandria's *Dialogue on the Incarnation of the Only-Begotten*, was first published in Greek in Migne's PG 75:1189-1253; and subsequently in critical edition and French translation by M. De Durand, *Cyrille d'Alexandrie: Deux Dialogues Christologiques, Sources Crétiennes,* v. 97 (Paris, 1964), pp. 188-301.[9] Additionally, a Modern Greek translation has been used for comparing pivotal theological and Christological terms. The Modern Greek translation was published by the University of Thessaloniki in Τὸ Παλίμψηστον 1998, p 223. The Modern Greek

---

[9] Cyril and Georges-Matthieu de Durand, *Deux dialogues christologiques* (Paris: Du Cerf, 1964).

edition was accompanied by analysis and commentary by Dr. Chrysostomos Stamoulis.[10] The translation used is the result of composition derived from a comparative reading of three critical editions of the work that used the entire manuscript tradition. In this way an attempt was made to reduce errors and faithfully attempt to present the original meaning.

This dialogue was first published by J. Aubert in 1638 and was solely based on the Manacensis Graecus 398 manuscript of the 10th century.[11] It was also published for the first time in Latin in Bonaventura Vulcanio in 1605.[12] In 1863, J. P. Migne published a critical edition of the J. Aubert edition which can be found in PG 75, 1189-1253.

In 1877, P. E. Pusey republished the dialogue using a different set of manuscripts consisting of the 14th century Vaticanus Gracus 596 fol. 314r – 349v[13], Vatopedinus 390 fol. 250c – 273[14],

---

[10] Κυρίλλου Ἀλεξανδρείας, Περί τῆς ενανθρωπήσεως τοῦ Μονογενοῦς (Α.Σ. 2), εκδόσεις "Το Παλίμψηστον", Θεσσαλονίκη 1998, σ. 223.

[11] Ignaz Hardt, Johann Christoph von Aretin, and Königliche Hof- und Staatsbibliothek (München), *Catalogus codicum manuscriptorum Graecorum Bibliothecae Regiae Bavaricae IV* (Monachii, 1806), 230–232.

[12] Cyrille, *Deux dialogues christologiques*, 165.

[13] Eugène Müntz, *La Bibliothèque du Vatican au XVe siècle d'après des documents inédits; contributions pour servir à l'histoire de l'humanisme* (Paris: E. Thorin, 1887), 82, 238, 324.

[14] Sophronios Eustratiades and Arkadios, *Catalogue of the Greek Manuscripts in the Library of the Monastery of Vatopedi on Mt. Athos* (Cambridge: Harvard Univ. Press [u.a.], 1924), 74–75.

and Mediceus Laurentianus Plut 35 fol. 146r – 165c[15]. In 1964, G. M. Durand published a critical edition of the text with an introduction and a commentary which is the main edition on which this English translation is based.

The Author

Born in Alexandria, Cyril became bishop of Alexandria after his uncle Theophilus (fl. 385-412). Although he was born to a prominent and highly dynamic family, very little information is known about his youth until the time he assumed the patriarchal throne.[16] Nonetheless, one of the earliest accounts about the life of Cyril was that he "accompanied his uncle to the Synod of Oak which deposed John Chrysostom."[17] After spending a period of time learning in the wilderness, he was ordained to the diaconate and later to the priesthood by his uncle. On the 18th of October 412, three days after the departure of Theophilus, he was voted as patriarch against the group favoring Archdeacon Timothy.[18] His early career (412-428) was dedicated to the exposition of the

---

[15] Biblioteca medicea laurenziana and Angelo Maria Bandini, *Catalogus codicum manuscriptorum Bibliothecae Mediceae Laurentianae varia continens opera Graecorum Patrum* (Florence: Typis Caesareis, 1764), 59–60.

[16] Hans Von Campenhausen, *The Fathers of the Church* (Hendrickson Publishers, Incorporated, 1998), 146.

[17] Frances M Young, *From Nicaea to Chalcedon: a Guide to the Literature and Its Background* (Philadelphia: Fortress Press, 1983), 242.

[18] Panagiotis C Christou, *Greek patrology IV* (Thessaloniki: Patriarchal Institute for Patristic Studies, 1989), 340.

Scriptures and the refutation of the heretics and the unbelievers.[19] Thus he wrote commentaries on the entire Bible and profound treatises about the cardinal dogma of Christianity, the Holy Trinity. The second period of his episcopate, 428-433 was more intense and fruitful than any other and was marked by his opposition to Nestorius of Constantinople. He rallied the whole Church to the discussions on the second cardinal dogma of Christianity, the incarnation of the Logos/Son of God. Cyril emerged as the greatest Christology teacher of the Church, whose teaching was to dominate decisively how the Church understands Christ. Cyril's stand was strengthened by his alliance with the Church of Rome and led to the summoning of the Council of Ephesus (431), which ended with Nestorius' condemnation.[20]

Cyril has been, on many occasions, accused of being a bully who committed many crimes. There were many allegations against him, particularly those accusing him with political attacks against Orestes, the murder of Hypatia, and the deportation of Jews from the City of Alexandria.[21] However, this trend started in history with the accounts of Socrates who had a great deal of hatred towards

---

[19] Campenhausen, *The Fathers of the Church*, 146.
[20] C. Papadouplous, "Saint Cyril of Alexandria. Alexandria: Patriarchal Press, 1933.
[21] Young, *From Nicaea to Chalcedon*, 243–244.

Cyril.²² This is perhaps why one could argue that he was not even fair in his account as a historian, simply because he could have been reporting hostile rumors circulating in Constantinople as opposed to witnessing the truth personally in the streets of Alexandria. At any rate, these events mentioned by Socrates allegedly occurred in the first four years of Cyril's episcopate and cannot be substantiated as the rest of Cyril's years as a bishop were quite peaceful apart from theological battles.²³ Contrary to western scholarship which adopts the historical accounts of Socrates, St. Cyril's good character and sainthood cannot only be seen through his theological treatises and dogmatic works, but also be easily glimpsed from the following excerpt which he wrote in one of his letters:

> I love peace; there is nothing that I detest more than quarrels and disputes. I love everybody, and if I could heal one of the brethren by losing all my possessions and goods, I am willing to do so joyfully; because it is concord that I value most ... But there is question of the faith and of a scandal which concerns all the churches of the Roman Empire ... The sacred doctrine is entrusted to us ... I am ready to endure with tranquility all blame, all humiliations, all injuries provided that the faith is not endangered. I am filled with love for Nestorius; nobody loves him more than I do ... If, in accordance with Christ's commandment, we must love our very enemies

---

²² Fulbert Cayré, *Manual of Patrology and History of Theology: Transl. by H. Howitt. 1. 1.u.2. Books. 1935. 1. 1.u.2. Books. 1935.* (Paris: Desclée, 1935), 21.

²³ Young, *From Nicaea to Chalcedon*, 244.

themselves, is it not natural that we should be united in special affection to those who are our friends and brethren in the priesthood? But when the faith is attacked, we must not hesitate to sacrifice our life itself. And if we fear to preach the truth because that causes us some inconvenience, how, in our gatherings, can we chant the combats and triumphs of our holy martyrs?[24]

The last period of Cyril's life, 433-444 was reasonably peaceful, though he had to explain his teaching to critics from both the Alexandrine and the Antiochene sides. He wrote several dogmatic writings during this period and continued to enlighten the Church with his profound Festal Letters and Paschal Homilies. Cyril is one of the most distinguished theologians of the early Church, recognized by his contemporaries and his successors in the East (Chalcedonian and non-Chalcedonian Orthodox) and in the West (Roman Catholics and Protestants). He is the first father to establish firmly the patristic argument, which appeals to the earlier fathers of the Church for the right understanding of the apostolic preaching and the gospel of Christ.[25]

---

[24] Alexander Kerrigan, *St. Cyril of Alexandria, Interpreter of the Old Testament* (Roma: Pontificio Istituto Biblico, 1952), 7.

[25] Ibid.

St. Cyril's Works

Cyril was a prolific writer who had an extensive knowledge of the sciences, philosophies, the Scriptures and the Fathers, especially Athanasius and the Cappadocians. Cyril was not, however, a "literary parrot like the later Byzantine scholastics."[26] The exegetical works of St. Cyril were not merely means of formal commentaries, but a "thematic treatment aimed at presenting what might be called a 'biblical theology', worked out in relation to the five books of the law."[27] Cyril also wrote many *Homilies* and Letters. More specifically, the works of St. Cyril include:

1. **Exegetical Works:**

On worship in Spirit and in Truth (PG 68:131-1126). This work represents an exposition of the Gospel in comparison with the Law (Pentateuch) of the Old Testament. This work consists of 17 books presented in the form of a dialogue between St. Cyril and Palladius. Quasten breaks the 17 books into a series of ideas discussing the fall of Adam and Eve (book 1), justification through Jesus Christ (books 2 and 3), the Human Will (books 4 and 5), salvation (books 6 – 8), ecclesiology (books 9 – 13), spiritual worship (books 14 – 16), and finally the feasts of the Jews (book 17). This

---

[26] Young, *From Nicaea to Chalcedon*, 246.

[27] Ibid., 247.

work was presumably written any time between 412 and 429 A.D.[28] In this work, "St. Cyril shows that the 'law and the prophets are not abolished but perfected, since the rites practiced in a material way by the Jews find their continuation in the spiritual adoration that the Christians pay to God; the Jewish observances were the figure and the shadow of the new worship."[29]

The following five works which are known to be contemporaneous with *De Adoratione in Spiritu* are expositions of select Pentateuch passages:

Glaphyra (=Selections) on Genesis (PG 69: 13-386).

Glaphyra (=Selections) on Exodus (PG 69: 385-538).

Glaphyra (=Selections) on Leviticus (PG 69: 539-590).

Glaphyra (=Selections) on Numbers (PG 69: 589-642).

Glaphyra (=Selections) on Deuteronomy (PG 69: 643-678).

Cayré outlines that the purpose of the *Glaphyra* is "to determine all the figures of Christ contained in the books of Moses."[30] Therefore, St. Cyril only studied the passages in that reflected these figures of Christ.

Fragments from the Commentary on the Books of Kings (PG 69: 679-698).

Exegesis of the Psalms (PG 69: 717-1274).

Fragments from the Commentary on the Song of Songs (PG 69:1277-1294).

---

[28] Johannes Quasten and Italy) Istituto patristico Augustinianum (Rome, *Patrology* (Westminster, Md.: Christian Classics, 1986), 121.

[29] Cayré, *Manual of Patrology and History of Theology*, 24.

[30] Ibid.

Exegesis of Isaiah (PG 70: 9-1450).

Fragments from the Commentaries on Jeremiah, Baruch, Ezekiel and Daniel (PG 70: 1451-1462).

Exegesis of Hosea (PG 71: 9-328, crit. ed. Pusey 1868 vol. 1).

Exegesis of Joel (PG 71: 327-408, crit. ed. Pusey 1868 vol. 1).

Exegesis of Amos (PG 71: 407-582, crit. ed. Pusey 1868 vol. 1).

Exegesis of Obadiah (PG 71: 581-596, crit. ed. Pusey 1868 vol. 1).

Exegesis of Jonah (PG 71: 597-638, crit. ed. Pusey 1868 vol. 1).

Exegesis of Micah (PG 71: 639-776, crit. ed. Pusey 1868 vol. 1).

Exegesis of Navy (PG 71: 775-844, crit. ed. Pusey 1868 vol. 2).

Exegesis of Habakkuk (PG 71: 843-944, crit. ed. Pusey 1868 vol. 2).

Exegesis of Zephaniah (PG 71: 943-1022, crit. ed. Pusey 1868 vol. 2).

Exegesis of Haggai (PG 71: 1021-1062, crit. ed. Pusey 1868 vol. 2).

Exegesis of Zechariah (PG 72: 9-276, crit. ed. Pusey 1868 vol. 2).

Exegesis of Malachi (PG 72: 275-364, crit. ed. Pusey 1868 vol. 2).

Exegesis of Matthew's Gospel (PG 72: 365-470, crit. ed. Reuss 1957).

Exegesis of Luke's Gospel (PG 72: 475-950, crit. ed. Sickenberger 1909, Reuss 1957, Syriac vers. Smith 1858, Wright 1874). This exegesis which is preserved in a fairly trustworthy Syriac translation was composed after 429 A.D. and is more pastoral in nature than theological.[31]

Exegesis of John's Gospel (PG 73: 9-1056 and 74: 9-756, crit. ed. Pusey 1872, vols. i-iii).

Fragments from the Commentary on the Acts (PG 74: 757-774, crit. ed. Pusey 1872, vol. iii: 441-451).

Exegesis of the Epistle to the Romans (PG 74: 773-856, crit. ed. Pusey

---

[31] Ibid., 25.

1872, vol. iii: 174-248).

Exegesis of the 1st Epistle to the Corinthians (PG 74: 855-916, crit. ed. Pusey 1872, vol. iii: 249-319).

Exegesis of the 2nd Epistle to the Corinthians (PG 74: 915-952, crit. ed. Pusey 1872, vol. iii: 320-361).

Fragments from the Commentary on the Epistle to the Galatians and Colossians (PG 74: 951-952).

Exegesis of the Epistle to the Hebrews (PG 74: 953-1004, crit. ed. Pusey 1872, vol. iii: 362-423).

Fragments from the Commentaries on the Catholic Epistles of James, I & II Peter, I John and Jude (PG 1007-1038, crit. ed. Pusey 1872, vol. iii: 441-451).

2. Dogmatic Works:

Book of Treasures on the Holy and Consubstantial Trinity (PG 75: 9-656).

On the Holy and Consubstantial Trinity, Seven Orations (APG 75: 657-1124; cf. crit. ed. by de Durand, SC vols. i-iii, 1976, 1977, 1978).

On the Holy and Life-giving Trinity (PG 75: 1147-1190 (it is not Cyril's but belongs to Theodoret).

On the Incarnation of the Only-Begotten and that there is One Christ and Lord (PG 75: 1189 1254, crit. ed. Pusey 1865, vol. vii: 11-153, and de Durand SC 1964, pp. 188-301).

That Christ is One (PG 75: 1253-1362, crit. ed. Pusey 1865 tom. vii: 334-424, de Durand SC 1964, pp. 302-515, Ethiopic text and German translation Weischer 1977).

On the Incarnation of the Only-Begotten (PG 75:1369-1412, crit. ed. Schwartz ACO I, 5, i 184-215 and 219-231, Pusey 1865 tom. vi: 498-579, Armenian Text with English translation Conybeare 1907, Latin version PL 48: 1005-1048).

On the Incarnation of God the Logos and Son of the Father (PG 75: 1413-1420, crit. ed. Schwartz ACO I, 5, i 3-6) [dubious].

On the Incarnation of the Lord (PG 75: 1419-1478 [according to Ehrhardt it does not belong to Cyril but to Theodoret].

Pentabiblos (Five-fold) Objection Against the Blasphemies of Nestorius (PG 76:9-248, crit. ed. Pusey 1875 tom. vi: 54-239 and Schwartz ACO I, i, 6 13-106).

Dialogue with Nestorius that the Holy Virgin is Theotokos and not Christotokos, (PG 76: 2249-256) [According to Nau (1910) this is a later work containing an authentic Nestorius' part and an inauthentic Cyrillic part].

An Oration against those who are unwilling to confess the Holy Virgin as Theotokos, (PG 76: 255-292) [According to de Durand (1964) this is not an authentic Cyrillic work].

Apologeticus in defense of the Twelve Chapters to the Bishops of the East, (PG 76: 315-386, crit. ed. Pusey (1875) 260-386 and Schwartz ACO, I, i, 7: 33-65).

Letter to Euoptius, on the Objection raised by Theodoret on the Twelve Chapters (PG 76: 385-452, crit. ed. Pusey vi (1875) 384-497 and Schwartz ACO I, i, 6: 110-146. For a Latin version see PL 48: 969-1001 and Schwartz ACO I,5: 142-165, 249-287).

Apologeticus, to the Most Pious King (PG 76: 453-488, crit. ed. Pusey vii (1977) 425-456 and Schwartz ACO I, i, 3: 75-90).

In defence of the venerable Religion of the Christians in view of the opinion of the Emperor Julian who is included among the atheists, (PG 76: 503-1064, crit. ed. Newmann 1880).

Against the Anthropomorphites, (PG 76: 1065-1132) [According to Pusey this is a composite work consisting of three Cyrillic Epistles: a) To Kalosirios of Arsinoe (PG 76: 1065-1077), b) to Tiberios the Deacon (PG 76: 1077-1120) and c) On Solutions of Dogmas (Pusey iii (1872) 603-607, 567-602, 547-566), to which a portion from Gregory of Nyssa's homily "On the Birth of Christ" (PG 46: 1129-

1137=PG 76: 1121-1132). According to Chrys. Stamoulis (Thessaloniki 1993) the composition is Cyril's].

Prosphonetikos, On the Orthodox Faith to the Most Pious King Theodosius, (PG 76: 1133-1200, crit. ed. Pusey vii (1877) 1-152 and Schwartz ACO I,i,7 42-72. Also de Durand (1964) and Weischer (1973). De Durand sees a connection between this text and the other one on the Incarnation (PG 75: 1189-1284).

Prosphonetikos to the Most Pious Queens, (PG 76: 1201-1336, crit. ed. Pusey vii (1877) 154-262, and Schwartz ACO I, i, 1: 62-118).

Second Prosphonetikos to the Most Pious Queens on the Orthodox Faith, (PG 76: 1335-1420, crit. ed. Pusey vii (1877) 263-333, and Schwartz ACO I,i,5: 26-61).

Fragments from lost Dogmatic works: 1) *On the defectiveness of the Synagogue*, 2) *On not offering for the departed*, 3) *Against the Synousiasts (Apollinarists)*, and 4) *Against Diodore and Theodore*, (PG 76: 1321-1454, crit. ed. Pusey iii (1872) 541-544).

3. Epistles:

Epistles 1-88, (PG 77: 9-390) [Epistles 1-32 refer to the outbreak of the Nestorian controversy. Epistles 33-65 refer to John of Antioch and the Easterners. Epistles 66-74 refer to the expansion of Nestorianism. Epistles 77-79 and 85 refer to administrative matters. Epistle 81 refers to Origen, Epistle 82a, to the Messalians/Euchites. Epistles 75 and 76 refer to exegetical issues but the latter is Basil's (Ep. 260). Epistles 86-88 are pseudepigraphic. Schwartz added 4 new ones: ACO I,i,7 140-142, 152-153, 162-163 and published the Greek original of Epistles 32 and 33. Finally Divjak recovered a correspondence between Cyril and Augustine).

Festal Epistles 1-30, (PG 77: 391-982), which cover the period AD 414-442.

Various Homilies, (PG 77: 981-1116) which were delivered in this order: 5, 2, 1, 6, 7, 4, 11, 20, 21, 3, 16, 15, 10.

4. **Disputed Works:**

Oration on the death of the Three Holy Youth and of the all-wise Daniel, (PG 77: 1117-1118)

A Book on the All-Holy Trinity (PG 77: 1119-1174), which presents many parallels with John Damascene (Mahe 1923) and presents a problem of ownership.

Collection of OT verses interpreted anagogically, briefly and succinctly collected for the sake of clarity from Cyril, Maximus and other exegetes, (PG 77: 1175-1290).

St. Cyril's Liturgy, (PG 77: 1291-1308).

Language and Theological Significance

As aptly pointed out by G. M. Durand in his French edition, the Dialogue Cyril does not defend any theological system, but responds with critical and perceptive clarity on disparate challenges of heretics that alter the Divine-human person of Christ and deny the hope of salvation. The Dialogue, although a single piece of work, can essentially be divided into three parts: Introduction, Report on the Christological heresies made by Hermias, and finally a refutation of the heretical Christology as outlined by St. Cyril of Alexandria.

Cyril resorts to the use of systematic thought to refute the heretics' main arguments and their discrepancies to prove their unorthodox Christology which they use to eliminate the real sense of salvation of the members of the ecclesiastical body. The whole struggle of the Church becomes the reality of the incarnation, the reality of Christ, and the reality of salvation. Cyril uses specific terminology to convey his theological meanings and Christological refutations. The following few lines will attempt to highlight and analyze some of those terms and their theological significance.

Similar to his other dialogues, Cyril uses (κατά φύσιν) to establish the consubstantiality of the Son with the Father, to affirm that the Son is true God of true God and not merely κτίσμα or ποίημα "created or made". Although (κατά φύσιν) is traditionally translated "according to nature", I believe a more accurate translation that is rooted in the Alexandrian understanding of the word is "according to reality".[32] Furthermore, Cyril discusses how human attributes are ascribed to the Son but are not true to his nature as he is God, but instead that these human characteristics could be ascribed to Christ (τη μετά σαρκός οικονομία) "by the economy with flesh". Cyril then uses this notion to assert that Christ uses this union for the sanctification of humanity which is rather an integral part of his soteriological thought. The Son of God himself does not need sanctification but humanity is sanctified in him. Perhaps this notion presents us with Cyril's approach to deification.

Moreover, the notion of "hypostatic union" in Cyril's language is intended to express the idea of "the concurrence of the divine and the human form in one person, so that whether as God or as man or

---

[32] See G. W. H. Lampe, A Patristic Greek Lexicon (Oxford; New York: Oxford University Press, 1969), 1498.

as both Christ constituted a single objective reality (hypostasis)".³³ Additionally, Cyril's use of the Greek term (οικονομία) portrayed his strong belief that "God was learning and deciding in his manhood "economically" – that is to say, within the sphere and terms of the incarnation – what He already knew and had decided from all eternity as God." ³⁴ This notion is perhaps more evident in one of his other work where he writes "Sometimes He discourses as man, economically and manwise; sometimes He makes His utterances with divine authority, as God."³⁵

Like his predecessor, Cyril uses the language and theology of St. Athanasius. He uses the word (κένωσις) "emptying" to highlight Christ's voluntary act of incarnation which does not affect his divine substance but subjects him to human limitations in his earthly life. "Like Athanasius, Cyril distinguishes between divine and human attributes in the context of the anti-Arian argument, but it is noticeable that already he is insisting on the subjection of the Logos to human conditions in the incarnation, and occasionally criticizing the tendency to divide the Christ."³⁶ Instead, Cyril uses the phrase (περὶ τούτων ἐννοίαις καὶ τὴν ἀμφοῖν εἰς ἑνότητα συνδρομήν) "both

---

[33] George Leonard Prestige, *Fathers and Heretics: Six Studies in Dogmatic Faith with Prologue and Epilogue* (London; New York: Society for Promoting Christian Knowledge ; Macmillan, 1940), 157.

[34] Ibid, 158.

[35] *Ad Succens* I, 137b.

[36] Young, *From Nicaea to Chalcedon*, 254.

coming together into union" to perhaps denote that he accepts the term "two natures" if spoken (δύο φύσεις τη θεωρία μόνη), that is "in thought only".[37] This perhaps further affirms his understanding that Christ is One REALITY (φύσις), which harbors "two natures" (*natura*).

Cyril is again very keen in his presentation to emphasize One Son of God who is our Lord Jesus Christ, both before and after the (σάρκωσις) "enfleshment" who is (προαιώνιος) "before the ages". Cyril then highlights that Christ is born from the virgin and has (ἴδια) "his own" flesh. Cyril refutes the idea of (σύγκρασις) "mixture or alteration" and instead insists that Christ united to himself (σῶμα εψυχωμενον ψυχή νοερά) "a body ensouled with a rational soul" taking the form of a servant without actually doing so in his essence. "What Cyril plainly meant was the concurrence of the divine and human forms in one person, so that whether as God or as man or as both Christ constituted a single objective reality (hypostasis)."[38]

Cyril's language and its theological significance were not only present in the above expositions of faith and dogma, but also in his refutations of certain heresies. For example, he denied the usage of the phrase (ἄνθρωπος θεοφόρος) "a God-bearing man" to deny the idea

---

[37] See "Joint Commission for Theological Dialogue between the Orthodox Church and the Oriental Orthodox Churches" (1991), p. 186 from the meeting held at the Orthodox Centre of Ecumenical Patriarchate, Chambesy, Geneva on 23-28 September 1990. This phrase is used by Cyril in his letter to John of Antioch and his letters to Acacius of Melitene (pages 77, 184-201), and to Eulogius (pages 224-228) and to Succensus (pages 77, 228-245).

[38] Prestige, *Fathers and Heretics*, 157.

that Christ did not assume an independent human being.

It is also possible that Cyril might have relied on this very dialogue in his later refutations in Nestorius as there are multiple sentence formations, phrases and expressions that are used in this dialogue and later repeated in his work titled "*Ad Nestorius*". An example of this language is evident in his use of the phrase "to suppose and think with others, by boundless sluggishness, that the Word of God refused the birth from the Holy Virgin, despised our nature and preferred to be transformed into a flesh from the earth, these are the people who blaspheme concerning the economy and allow themselves to scorn the plans of God."[39] And further "And not that He put on the flesh alone, impoverished of a rational soul, but He was born of a woman in truth, and became man."[40] These two excerpts could be easily compared with the phrase "we do not say that the nature of the Word was changed in order to become flesh, not that it was transformed into a complete man of soul and body: but rather this, that the Word united to Himself in an objective reality, ineffably and incomprehensibly, flesh ensouled with a rational soul, and thus became man."[41]

Finally, one of the most important aspects of Cyril's writings is his ability to maintain and distinguish theologically between what

---

[39] See p. 37.

[40] See p. 60.

[41] *Ad Nest.* 3, 70A.

can be studied and what is beyond all understanding. "There are dangers, subtle and profound, in a theology which overelaborates its dogmas; which concentrates notice too much on secondary issues, so distracting the mind from God rather than making him the center of attention."[42] Cyril's proper use of apophatic theology avoids those dangers and is perhaps one of his strongest tools against his opponents. The use of apophatic language in Cyril's writing can be traced throughout this dialogue; he uses words like ($ἀπορρήτως$) "beyond understanding" to mark the point where he will not venture any longer, he says for example: "God, on the contrary, whose existence is beyond all understanding, above all alteration or corruption is also superior to any change."[43]

Emmanuel Gergis

---

[42] Prestige, *Fathers and Heretics*, 170.

[43] See p. 38.

The Translation

ST. CYRIL – In your opinion, do we give our dialogue on the divinity of the Only-Begotten Son proper attention and sufficient consideration?

HERMIAS – Yes, absolutely.

ST. CYRIL – As a matter of fact, I suppose no one has given a meticulous examination – at least that is what seems to me. And you, Hermias, what do you say?

HERMIAS – I would like to praise appropriately what is correct and refined.

ST. CYRIL – Leaving all that aside, without lingering any further, do you want to speak about the Incarnation of the Only-Begotten Son? Let us try to discern as clearly as possible regarding this mystery, at least insofar as it is possible for those who are confused, who know in part, to the extent of the gifts "of the supply of the Spirit"[44], as the divine Paul wrote.

---

[44] Phil. 1:19.

HERMIAS – Very true, because "no one can say, Jesus is Lord, except by the Holy Spirit".[45] And no one anathematizes Jesus except by Beelzebub.[46] Well, since you think I should consider the conversation and undertake such a difficult and insufferable task, you understand that first and foremost you are doing me a favor: for it is my greatest pleasure to examine Christ's accurate and unadulterated doctrine, which is free from reproach. For different views have intoxicated some, and indeed have caused their heads to be turned by many opinions and they have disfigured the prophesies of the Old and New Testaments.

ST. CYRIL – There is nothing, dear friend, that these fools have not tried, they rushed as fast as they could "into the snare of Hades"[47], as it is written, and the snare of death, "understanding neither what they say, nor the things which they affirm".[48] What are the rumors of each one and their nonsense fables, can you explain to us, my dear noble one?

HERMIAS – Absolutely: some have dared to declare that the man who is the Word of God has appeared, but did not, indeed, possess the flesh taken from the Virgin. They tell the lie that the Mystery

---

[45] 1 Cor. 12:3; this verse is perhaps used in reference to the Orthodox notion of noetic θεωρία as means of apprehending God as opposed to philosophical categories of *gnosiology* that attempt to comprehend the totality of God.

[46] Mat. 12:24.

[47] Prov. 9:18.

[48] 1 Tim. 1:7.

was only an appearance. Others, arguing that they are ashamed to appear worshipping a man, refuse to honor with the utmost glory a terrestrial body. From their excessive ignorance, being sick with some false and corrupt vigilance, they say that the Word who is Begotten of God the Father was turned into a creature of bones, nerves and flesh upon the birth of Emmanuel from the Virgin. These miserable ones are laughable. They count as inappropriate this most noble and divine economy.

Still, others have believed God the Word who is co-eternal with the Father, to be a late-comer[49] and to be called into existence just at the same time of the beginning of His birth in the flesh. Others have reached such a degree of insanity and impiety to declare the Word of God without hypostasis; simply a word – in the sense that a word is uttered – which would then become a man. These are Marcellus[50] and Photinus[51].

---

[49] The notion of before or after cannot be applied to the divine persons as it is only appropriate in talking about creatures who experience chronological time or χρόνος. Divine "time" or καιρός is an ontological state of being. χρόνος represents the chronological human time which is measured by the succession of seconds, minutes, days, weeks, months, and years, while the καιρός represents divine time which is measured by whether a person is in the presence of divinity or not. See Ben Witherington, *The Problem with Evangelical Theology: Testing the Exegetical Foundations of Calvinism, Dispensationalism, and Wesleyanism* (Waco, Texas: Baylor University press, 2005), 124.

[50] One of the bishops present at the councils of Ancyra and Nicaea who was an extreme opponent to Arianism, but later made erroneous Sabellian statements and was later condemned by many theologians including St. Athanasius and Eusebius of Caesarea who wrote two works against him. Arendzen, J. (1910). Marcellus of Ancyra. In The Catholic Encyclopedia. New York: Robert Appleton Company. Retrieved September 26, 2013 from New Advent: http://www.newadvent.org/cathen/09642a.htm

Others believe that the Only-Begotten actually became man; He came in the flesh, but did not assume that flesh which is fully animated by a rational soul and endowed with an intellect like ours. Imagining a complete seal on the unity between the Word of God and the temple from the Virgin, they say that the Word dwelt in the temple; and the temple was the body that assumed and played the role of the rational and intellectual soul. Still others have adopted doctrines opposed to those and contradicted these opinions, maintaining strongly that Emmanuel is combined and mingled with the Word of God and a rational soul and body, which is to say, of an absolutely complete humanity. But they too have not kept an entirely sound and blameless doctrine regarding Him. In fact, they divide into two the One Christ, introducing into Him a very brutal separation, representing virtually Him as divided: one is, what they say, a complete man born from the Virgin, the other, the Word of God the Father. Separating God's nature from that of the flesh and wishing to adhere to their distinction. How would there be no offense against the true doctrine? For the flesh and the divine nature are not the same. But they separate asunder the one as a human individual, and the other they name as God and truly Son, and want to be called Christians! Here are their own words elsewhere, in

---

[51] Bishop of Sirmium who was also condemned for Sabellianism as Marcellus. See Chapman, J. (1911). Photinus. In The Catholic Encyclopedia. New York: Robert Appleton Company. Retrieved September 26, 2013 from New Advent: http://www.newadvent.org/cathen/12043a.htm

certain fantasies they have written on these topics: "One," they dared to say, "is inherently by nature, the true Son and Word of God the Father, the other is son by sharing the name with the Son." Still further: "The Word of God is not flesh, but He took hold of a man." Indeed, the Only-Begotten is literally Himself the Son of God who created the universe; the man he assumed, on the contrary, is not the Lord by nature, and is called the son, because of the true Son of God who assumes the same name.

Indeed, the phrase: "No one knows the Son except through the Father"[52], mandates that He is truly the Son and from the nature of the Father. On the contrary, the words of Gabriel: "Do not be afraid, Mary, you have found favor with God, and behold you will conceive in your womb and bring forth a son, and shall call His Name Jesus"[53] apply to a human. Behold what these people are saying. As for us, we do not think so. How so? Because the heterodox ideas do not convince us to leave the straightforward path or proceed in the oblique path without a purpose. You, however, proceed with your discourse to convince me of the best possible doctrine, for I am quite willing to listen and be educated.

ST. CYRIL – What a heavy task and an unbearable burden! Do you not know, dear friend, who decided to respond to each of them in a

---

[52] Mat. 11:27.
[53] Luke 1:30–31.

long and detailed response and spend such a long time? This would barely succeed after a great price and a difficult effort.

HERMIAS – That's true.

Against Docetism: True Flesh and True Body

ST. CYRIL – Let us leave here, if you will, any idea of prolonged and subtle rebuttal, let us in each case give a very brief review, and come, let us begin before all others with the Docetists.[54]

"You are mistaken," they tell us, "because you do not know the Scriptures and the great Mystery of Godliness," that is to say, the Christ, "Who was manifested in the flesh, justified in the Spirit, seen by angels, preached among the nations, believed on in the world, taken up in glory".[55] I think our opponents have labeled with infamy, the old teachings, and called preachers of the economy liars, those to whom Christ Himself said: "Go therefore and make disciples of all nations".[56] Or, if they dare not do so, they will be deciding to think appropriately about Christ, leaving their absurdity, clinging firmly to the Sacred Scriptures and springing in the unerring path of the saints, walking on it towards the truth. For the mystery of godliness, in my opinion, cannot be to us other than the

---

[54] St. Cyril addressed Docetism previously in his Commentary on the Gospel of John, chapter 12.

[55] 1 Tim. 3:16.

[56] Mt. 28:19.

Word of God the Father appearing in the flesh. For He was born from the Holy Virgin, taking the form of a slave, and in response the angels celebrated His birth saying: "Glory to God in the highest, and on earth peace, goodwill toward men".[57] Thereby showing to the shepherds God the Word appearing in the flesh for us, they told them: "For unto you is born this day in the city of David a Savior, Who is Christ the Lord. And this will be a sign to you; you will find a Babe wrapped in swaddling clothes, lying in a manger".[58] But if this virginal birth and this manifestation in the flesh are true; how could it not be idle talk, how would it not be feeble nonsense, and how is it not empty madness to describe the name of this evident economy as an "appearance"? If this was a shadow and an apparition, and not true incarnation, then the Virgin has not given birth, the Word of God the Father did not assume "the seed of Abraham".[59] He did not become like His brethren. For our condition is not at all a shadow or an apparition, but we are in a visible and tangible body, clothed in this earthly flesh and subject to corruption and passions. Also, if the Word did not become flesh, He did not "aid those who are tempted"[60], for a shadow does not suffer; all that is to us truly comes to nothing. For whose back did He surrender for us? Or of

---

[57] Luke 2:14.

[58] Luke 2:11-12.

[59] Heb. 2:16.

[60] Heb. 2:18.

what kind is His subjecting of His cheeks to those that smote Him, enduring the bellows of the Jews? One Who was not manifest in the flesh, how should we think then He had hands and feet to deal with the nails? Or of what nature is the side, tell me, which Pilate's soldiers pierced where the Precious Blood mixed with water was flowing?[61] If it is necessary to speak beyond this, according to their words, it would be said that Christ neither died for us nor resurrected. Accept it as truth, faith would be empty without meaning[62], gone would be the Cross, the life and salvation of the world, the hope of those who have fallen asleep in faith would be destroyed.[63]

For this was the opinion of the blessed Paul: "For I delivered unto you first of all that which I also received, that Christ died for our sins according to the Scriptures; and that He was buried, and that He rose again the third day according to the Scriptures, and that He was seen by Cephas, then by the twelve. After that, He was seen by over five hundred brethren at once, of whom the greater part remain to the present, but some have fallen asleep. After that, He was seen by James, then by all the apostles. Then last of all He was seen by me also, as by one born out of due time", according to

---

[61] John 19:34.
[62] 1 Cor. 15:14.
[63] 1 Cor. 15:18.

his expression.⁶⁴ And again later: "Now if Christ is preached that He has been raised from the dead, how do some among you say that there is no resurrection of the dead? But if there is no resurrection of the dead, then Christ is not risen. And if Christ is not risen, then our preaching is empty, and your faith is also empty. Yes, and we are found false witnesses of God, because we have testified of God that He raised up Christ, Whom He did not raise up--if in fact the dead do not rise".⁶⁵ In fact, tell me then how a shadow could die? How then did the Father raise Christ if He was a shadow and an apparition and could not become captive and bound by death? Far from us then is their vomit! Their comments are rather fables and misbehavior of an impure imagination. For concerning these, the disciple formerly predicted to us, writing about the Savior: "Many false prophets have gone out into the world. By this you know the Spirit of God: Every spirit that confesses that Jesus Christ has come in flesh is of God: Every spirit that does not confess that Jesus Christ has come in the flesh is not of God. And this is the spirit of the Antichrist, which you have heard was coming, and is now already in the world".⁶⁶ And indeed, if He did not become man, He has not ascended in the flesh to God the Father in heaven, and He also cannot return from the heaven to us, which is to say then that

---

⁶⁴ 1 Cor. 15:3-7.

⁶⁵ 1 Cor. 15:12-15.

⁶⁶ 1 John 4:1-3.

CHRISTOLOGICAL DIALOGUE

He is a man and in the flesh. What I have said there is clear, do you not think so?

HERMIAS – Yes, absolutely.

He took Flesh without Change or Alteration to the Divinity

ST. CYRIL – To suppose and think with others, by boundless sluggishness, that the Word of God refused the birth from the Holy Virgin, despised our nature and preferred to be transformed into a flesh from the earth, these are the people who blaspheme concerning the economy and allow themselves to scorn the plans of God. For the Creator of all, the Word of God, rich in mercies, emptied Himself for us "was born a man, born from a woman"[67] so, "the children have partaken of flesh and blood," this we say, "He Himself likewise shared in the same, that through death He might destroy him who had the power of death, that is, the devil, and release those who through fear of death were all their lifetime subject to bondage".[68] Thus it is expressed in the Sacred Scriptures; these people, they stress the alleged impropriety of such excellent and wonderful design as though they were capable of inventing better, they even criticize the plans of Wisdom. We must not, they say, accuse the Only-Begotten Son of suffering birth by a woman in

---

[67] Phil. 2:7; Gal. 4:4.
[68] Heb. 2:14-15.

pain, thinking that the nature of the Word was transformed into a perishable body and born of the earth. They envision a change in Him Who cannot change. For the nature of God is fixed in His own good character, and His permanence is unshaken.

They object that if the nature is born in time, having been brought to existence, it will be then likely to suffer change: there is nothing in this realm that seems permissible or plausible; he whose existence had a beginning holds in himself the seed of inevitable change. God, on the contrary, whose existence is beyond all understanding, above all alteration or corruption is also superior to any change. For the very notion of His nature, so to speak, transcends and surpasses, as I know, all beings subject to becoming alive, in that immeasurable way. Similarly, all are subject to being created by Him; He is too high to be affected. Thus the divinity is unchangeable in goodness; the creatures change, transform, and are always near corruption. And this, the prophet Jeremiah knew well and philosophized about it best when he said to God that: "For you endure forever, and we perish utterly."[69]

---

[69] Baruch 3:33. As with the ancient tradition, the writings of a student are always attributed to the teacher. Biblical Scholars believe that Baruch was the student of Jeremiah, or at least that the writer of the book of Jeremiah is also the writer of the book of Baruch. It was, perhaps, common knowledge at the time of St. Cyril that Jeremiah was the teacher of Baruch and this is why he attributes this verse to Jeremiah even though it is mentioned in Baruch. This discipleship of Baruch to Jeremiah is mentioned in Jeremiah 45:1, 36:1-10 and again in 36:27-32. See Gigot, Francis. "Baruch." The Catholic Encyclopedia. Vol. 2. New York: Robert Appleton Company, 1907. Furthermore, this perhaps presents us with a solid proof that – at least until the time of St. Cyril – the Old Testament in the Christian

CHRISTOLOGICAL DIALOGUE

Indeed, Divinity is steadfast in His being, reigning forever and governing the universe, it is not tyrannized by all of the passions. As for us, having a nature that is most fleeting, and easily led astray with cares towards change and alteration, so "we perish utterly," that is to say that at every moment, at every instance, we are prey to corruption and change. Accordingly, the Deity is never exposed to losing its own stability under the influence of disturbances. However, the corruptible and changeable nature, that is to say, which is born, does not acquire the immutable essence. Also, the creature does not exult in the goodness of the divine nature as his own, under the penalty of being told if it is appropriate: "What do you have that you did not receive?"[70] And that the nature of the Word is unchangeable and entirely immutable, while creatures are entirely mutable, someone might very easily perceive through the words of this song by the blessed David, inspired by the Spirit saying: "The heavens will perish, but You will endure; Yes, they will all grow old like a garment; Like a cloak You will change them, And they will be changed. But You are the same, and Your years will have no end".[71] Now how has the Word of God remained the same even if it is true that He has abandoned His immovability and permanence and descended to become what He was not and become

---

tradition included what is today known as the deuterocanonical books as an integral part of its content.

[70] 1 Cor. 4:7.

[71] Ps. 101:26-28.

a flesh, made to be corrupted? Now, is this not idle talk even for the demented?

HERMIAS – Yes, absolutely.

True Birth from a Virgin

ST. CYRIL – Now it is time to oppose such nonsense and to say that it is even more ignorant: it would be absurd that even the flesh from the earth could rise one day somehow to the nature of the Divinity and become the same with the Essence (*ousia*) of the Being Who is above all beings. For if the Nature of the Godhead, as is the aberration of these people, has transformed Itself into the nature of the flesh, nothing yet prevents the lower bodily nature itself to rise up and become the Godhead and His supreme Essence. But we will not provide any credit to the insanities of these people; we will concentrate on the contrary, on the Holy Scriptures, and the Prophet who said: "Behold a virgin shall conceive and bear a Son and they shall call His Name Emmanuel".[72] And Blessed Gabriel confirms the prophecy and explains to the Virgin the declaration from on high: "Do not be afraid Mary," he says, "You will conceive in your womb and bring forth a son and shall call His Name Jesus".[73] So we believe that Emmanuel is truly born of a woman and,

---

[72] Is. 7:14.
[73] Luke 1:30-31.

thinking correctly, we do not put asunder the pride, the brightness and the worth of our nature.

HERMIAS – You speak well. For, the Only-Begotten Son did not lay hold of His own nature – it would not enhance our condition – nor that of the angels, "but of the seed of Abraham,"[74] according to what was written. It was thus and in no other way the salvation of our race which has fallen into corruption.

ST. CYRIL – What? No, not here too, Hermias!

HERMIAS – What are you talking about?

Begotten Before the Ages

ST. CYRIL – They virtually leave the inspired Scriptures to engage their minds with the spirits of error. In this they have fallen into ill-counsel and childish stupidity, as to imagine that the Creator of the ages, God the Word Who is co-eternal with God the Father came to be at the moment of His birth in the flesh, and they imagine that He is a late-comer, the One Who transcends all age and time. As if at the last moment and with great difficulty, at the Incarnation, God the Father has essentially brought together into being and existence a temple born of the Virgin and the One by Whom and in Whom are all things. Did they not reach the peak of evil, those who have given their hearing to this most obvious and disgusting old tale, who

---

[74] Heb. 2:16.

filled their minds with this blatant lie? Really "Their throat is an open sepulcher; with their tongues they have used deceit; the poison of asps is under their lips: whose mouth is full of cursing and bitterness".[75]

HERMIAS – I agree, the saying of the Psalmist is true.

ST. CYRIL – He by Whom all things are, was He not necessarily before them all?

HERMIAS – You speak well.

ST. CYRIL – What then do they do when John writes: "In the beginning was the Word, and the Word was with God, and the Word was God. He was in the beginning with God. All things were made through Him; and without Him nothing was made that was made".[76] And again: "That which was from the beginning, which we have heard, which we have seen with our eyes, which we have looked upon, and our hands have handled, of the Word of life--the life was manifested, and we have seen, and bear witness, and declare to you that eternal life, which was with the Father, and was manifested unto us".[77] Christ also Himself revealed before the Jews the antiquity of His own existence. For when they said: "You are

---

[75] Ps. 5:10; 139:4; 9:28.
[76] John 1:1-3.
[77] 1 John 1:1-2.

not yet fifty years old, and have you seen Abraham?"[78] He told them bluntly: "Most assuredly I say to you, Before Abraham was, I AM."[79] The Man for Whom "I" is used, which is bestowed upon no one – for whom "I AM" is clearly ascribed – how can we perceive a beginning to His birth? Or by what manner might these ones admit that He has ever been called into existence in a given moment, whose beginning is beyond all understanding? If someone should want to contradict these ones more leisurely, it would not be difficult for the words of the divinely-inspired Scriptures to divert the harm of the folly of these ones. But these ideas clearly suffer from a blatant defect and a deformity so enormous; I find it quite unnecessary to cure them.

HERMIAS – You speak well.

His True *Hypostasis*

ST. CYRIL – So let us go to another mistake akin to that which we have condemned. And indeed some alter the beauty of truth as they could falsify a genuine certainty, "Lift not up your horn on high; do not speak iniquity against God"[80], as it is written. They imagine the Only-Begotten Son to be nonexistent and non-subsisting, He does not exist in His own Hypostasis, but quite simply as a word, just a

---

[78] John 8:57.
[79] Ibid.
[80] Ps. 74:6.

word uttered by God, and Who, according to these miserable ones, had lived in a man. Thus, Jesus, according to them, has been created. They speak highly of all the saints, but not of God. However, as the disciple of Christ says in a letter: "Who is a liar but he who denies that Jesus is the Christ? He is antichrist who denies the Father and the Son. Whoever denies the Son does not have the Father either; he who acknowledges the Son has the Father also".[81] Each of the two actually did know the other, for both of them are in both, and each is known in the other both by us and by the holy angels. No one would inquire about whom the Father is if he mentally does not understand that the Father begat a Son. Therefore, one can say in confidence I suppose that if the Son is devoid of living, we would not think that the Father is in the realm of reality. Also, how is He still the Father, unless He truly begat? Or, if Him who is uncreated nor at all subsisting is born, the one who is begotten will be nothing. And indeed what is left is not the equivalent of nothingness; but is pure nothingness. As a result, God would be the Father of nothingness. But O noble ones, I myself should speak concerning these explanations, which for us are just flat nonsense! Or at any rate explain this saying: what is the extraordinary love that God the Father gives us? Even if He sends to us His Son, the Son Who according to you lacks existence, He has then given to us nothingness, and the Word was not made flesh, He

---

[81] 1 John 2:22-23.

has not suffered the precious Cross, He has not destroyed the power of death, He did not come to life. For if He is indeed nothing, and does not exist according to you, how would He go through all this? The word of Holy Scripture would have deceived the believers; the steadfastness of the faith would be reduced to nothing.

HERMIAS – God forbid!

ST. CYRIL – What? Did we indicate that the Son did not exist in the form of God, speaking of the same Image and character of the Begetter?

HERMIAS – So perfectly.

ST. CYRIL – And the images are like their Archetype?

HERMIAS – How could it be otherwise?

ST. CYRIL – So if the image is not from the hypostasis and if the model does not exist by itself, they must logically concede out of necessity that the image is also devoid of existence, and obviously dishonor the Image of the Archetype. They dare say, is it not true?

HERMIAS – Yes perfectly.

ST. CYRIL – And tell me. Philip, in his excessive zeal to learn about Christ, asked Him to be made worthy to see the Father, saying: "Lord, show us the Father, and it is sufficient for us"[82], then

---

[82] John 14:8.

is He someone Who does not exist and is not hypostasized?

HERMIAS – Someone Who exists, of course!

ST. CYRIL – If the Son were therefore nothing, since He has no existence – as is the uncontrolled audacity of these people – is this why He presents Himself to us as the Image and exact knowledge of the Father, saying: "Have I been with you so long, and yet you have not known me, Philip? He who has seen Me has seen the Father".[83] Do you not think that I am in the Father and the Father is in Me? I and the Father are One".[84]

It is impossible however, in my view, for someone to perceive that which exists in Him Who does not exist; nor form a notion of One Who exists as identical in every respect with the One Who is without existence. How then will the Father be in the Son and the Son, in return, in the Father? Or is it not true to say that, if the Word has no independent existence, the Father is also threatened, having in Himself nothingness and considered to exist in nothingness? In fact, what has absolutely no being is considered nonexistent.

HERMIAS – This logic cannot pass without resistance, because it is in itself sick with such a greatly unprecedented sickness; nevertheless, how absurd ($α\pi η χές$) is the dogma of our adversaries.

---

[83] John 14:9.
[84] John 10:38.

CHRISTOLOGICAL DIALOGUE

ST. CYRIL – One similarly wonders, how the Father created beings through the Son Who does not possess being. On the other hand, if someone inquired if it is preferable for beings to exist or not exist, in what sense would you answer?

HERMIAS – I would say it is better to exist. In fact, the Creator Who gives existence to those that do not exist, is called Very Good, and really is.

ST. CYRIL – You speak most well. Did you say this is indeed the nature of things? So the creature is better off than He through Whom all was called to be: One, supposedly, did not exist, the other exists.

HERMIAS – Blasphemy! "The Word of God is living and powerful"[85], as it is written. Moreover, He also says "I am the Life".[86]

ST. CYRIL – But one cannot think He is Life if He does not continue to be, yet in nature He is life, because He does not lie. Therefore, the claim that the Word of God cannot exist, is an outright lie, wishful thinking of utmost senselessness.

HERMIAS – Absolutely. To Moses He, Himself, asserted: "I am the ONE WHO IS".[87] He Who is true, how to imagine a time

---

[85] Heb. 4:12.
[86] John 14:6.
[87] Ex. 3:14.

without Him being steadfast in His own hypostasis? He Who truly exists, how can one conceive of Him not existing in His own saving hypostasis?

ST. CYRIL – As a result, do we have every reason to assert the profound ignorance of those who launch such assertions?

HERMIAS – Yes, certainly.

ST. CYRIL – No more, we shall not approve those others, Hermias, we who are duly trained to pursue the truth.

HERMIAS – What else?

Animated Flesh with a Rational Soul

ST. CYRIL – Those who say that the flesh united to the Word is deprived of a rational soul. Indeed, the flesh that the Word assumed through His coming to the world is said to not possess a perceptive movement, attributing the activity of the intellect and the soul to the Only-Begotten. Because they have feared, I do not know why, to confess that the Word was united perfectly with what man possesses, that is to say, that which is of the soul and body, at least according to human reason. Deeming fit the complete abandonment of the faith that is most ancient and from above, and ignorantly choosing to follow their own wishes only, and their human logic.

CHRISTOLOGICAL DIALOGUE

They truly think so, "more highly than one should think".[88]

HERMIAS – And what is their reason for holding such an opinion?

ST. CYRIL – I will explain. We say that "the Mediator between God and men"[89], according to the Scriptures, is formed of humanity such as ours and fully conforms to its definition and is the Son of God by nature, that is to say the Only-Begotten Son. We strongly confirm, furthermore, that a companionship and ineffable reconciliation unto union[90] between unequal and different natures was accomplished. We recognize, even then, one Christ, one Lord and one Son, Who is both in our minds as in reality, God and man. We constantly maintain the complete indissolubility of the Union (ενωσιν), believing the same Son to be both the Only-Begotten as well as the Firstborn (πρωτότοκον). Only-Begotten, as the Word of God the Father, coming forth (πεφηνότα) from His essence, He became man, "the Firstborn among many brethren"[91]. For just as [in fact] there is One God and Father from Whom are all things, in like manner there is One Lord Jesus Christ through Whom are all things. For we recognize that He is God by nature, the Word by

---

[88] Romans 12:3.

[89] 1 Tim 2:5.

[90] The usage of St. Cyril to the terms (σύνοδος συνδρομή) to refer to "companionship" is perhaps another indication that the writing of this text was before the Nestorian saga, as there was no doubt that the companionship St. Cyril is mentioning is not in its Nestorian sense but as he writes later "We constantly maintain the complete indissolubility of the Union (ενωσιν)".

[91] Rom. 8:29.

Whom everything is, the same Who became flesh (γέγονε σάρξ), that is to say, man.

HERMIAS – [Everything] you were saying is most correct.

ST. CYRIL – But the doctrines of those people do not coincide, certainly not, with those we bring on this subject! They themselves confessedly acknowledge only one Jesus Christ – and in this they think well – they exceedingly reject as impious any division of Emmanuel into two. But having stripped away the flesh from the rational human soul they say that the Word is united with it. They found reason for doing so in their view convincingly. Elements, they declare, which, in compound (κατα σύνθεσιν), contribute to the formation of a single being must be for something partial and incomplete, seeing Who being perfect by Himself, as one may say, in His own nature, has no need of a compounding of parts. Similarly, they say that it is unbefitting to admit that the flesh united with the Word is a perfect man, in order that even the synthesis, which is contemplated (νοοιτο) in the case of Christ, the Word Himself is clearly and blamelessly saved from it. Moreover, they say, if we declare that Emmanuel consists of a perfect man and of the Word begotten of the Father, the danger is not small, or rather, it now appears inevitable; we are obliged, even unwittingly, to think and speak of two sons and two Christs.

HERMIAS – And how do we answer those people?

CHRISTOLOGICAL DIALOGUE

Christ is One Reality

ST. CYRIL – First, it is not appropriate to distress with endless quibbling regarding a tradition of faith, so ancient, coming to us from the holy Apostles themselves, nor to submit to the extreme, things that exceed the intelligence, nor to intervene as arbitrators who arbitrate shamelessly, that such a thing is good, and another of a different kind would be otherwise truly better. But it is rather preferable to impart to the All-wise God the way of inspecting what is His own, and not arrogantly criticize the examined things of His that are good. We have indeed heard: "For My thoughts are not your thoughts, nor are your ways My ways, says the Lord. For as the heavens are higher than the earth, so are My ways higher than your ways, and My thoughts than your thoughts".[92]

Then they will find wisely their opinion is entirely pointless and what is captivating them is ignorant. If one were to choose to strip away the divine temple from the rational soul, the union will be broken in two, being incomplete, very much so. For it is agreed regarding the whole man, meaning both soul and, I say, body, that the flesh is only and according to itself a part of Him. But as for the Word of God, no one could possibly take Him as a part of anything, nor incomplete, my good friends! He is absolutely perfect in His own nature. Or, therefore, will there be a challenge between two

---

[92] Is. 55:8-9.

single and imperfect elements, the concourse between the perfect Word, and the imperfect flesh, compared to a man perfectly realizing the concept of His nature? Hence, how will there be a union into one of something perfect out of imperfect things, if it is out of the perfect Word and the imperfect flesh, in the same way that this union occurs between the intellect of the perfect man, and His complete nature.

In fact, we do not worship in any way two sons, and do not speak about two Christs, even though we believe that coming together (τὴν εἰς ἑνότητα συνδρομήν) into one between a perfect man and the Word of God was accomplished in Emmanuel. However, in the opinion they deem preferable, and when they speak of the flesh only or of the begotten Word of God, nothing could have persuaded them to separate the flesh from the Only-Begotten, and confess a duality of Christs: but we accept that Emmanuel is the one Lord Jesus Christ, and on this point at least they have managed to make sense. Similarly, if we say that the Word of God was brought together (συνενηνέχθαι) and united (ἡνῶσθαι) ineffably and beyond understanding (ἀπορρήτως) with a perfect man, Who is composed of a soul and a body, we shall not conceive of a duality of Sons, but only one and the same God in nature, coming from the essence of God the Father, became man in the fullness of time, was born of the Blessed Virgin, worshiped (προσκυνούμενον) by us and by the holy angels, in accordance with the Scriptures.

CHRISTOLOGICAL DIALOGUE

HERMIAS – Is that to say, therefore, if they were to claim that everything we needed, was the coming of the Only-Begotten among us, Who wanted to be seen by all the earthly beings, live commonly among the men and show us the way of the evangelical virtue, that He put on (ἠμπέσχετο) the flesh like ours in the economy? For to them, God's own nature is not visible.

ST. CYRIL – Being ignorant, they condemn the purpose (σκοπός)[93] of the Incarnation, and they understand nothing of the great Mystery of godliness (cf. 1 Tim. 3:16). If the taking flesh (σάρκωσις) has the sole purpose of being seen by those on earth, without bringing anything else to the human nature, how is this better and wiser than the opinion that the Docetists formulate? Those miserable ones, who, stripping away from the Word a body and an earthly flesh, they invent a myth, that He was seen on earth as a man, and so it happens, they evidently agree that He is the Author (εισηγητής) of all that is most beautiful. Or is it better that you say, if the Word of God has no use of human nature, and He became flesh, that He got rid of the impurity of the flesh (ακαθαρσίας σαρκικης), that He was given the appearance of the terrestrial body, and has thus reached the goal He had set?

HERMIAS – So, the meaning of His dwelling (επιδημίας), the mode

---

[93] St. Cyril here emphasizes that the purpose of the incarnation was not merely so that God would assume a human flesh, but that the true purpose is that of θέωσις where humanity is called to "partake of divine nature" (2 Peter 1:4).

of the Incarnation, [and] what it accomplished are what I wish to thoroughly learn.

ST. CYRIL – Come, my dear, educate yourself with the Sacred Scriptures, apply the eye of your intelligence to the words of the holy Apostles, and perceive with clarity what you are looking for! Thus the wise Paul, who had in himself the words of Christ, told us, "Inasmuch then as the children have partaken of flesh and blood, He Himself likewise shared in the same, that through death He might destroy him who had the power of death, that is, the devil, and release those who through fear of death were all their lifetime subject to bondage".[94] Elsewhere, he gives us another explanation saying: "For what the law could not do in that it was weak through the flesh, God did by sending His own Son in the likeness of sinful flesh, on account of sin: He condemned sin in the flesh, that the righteous requirement of the law might be fulfilled in us who do not walk according to the flesh but according to the Spirit".[95] Accordingly, is it not perfectly evident and without any obscurity to anyone, that the Only-Begotten became like us, that is to say a perfect man, to restore us from the corruption that was introduced [from the outside] in our earthly flesh, by means of the economy according to the union, –much like a dye gives color– descending into harmony of the law of life, taking His humanity, showing that

---

[94] Heb. 2:14-15.
[95] Rom. 8:3-4.

His own fixed and immutable nature is stronger than sin itself?

HERMIAS – That, in my opinion, is not confusing, for it carries within itself evidence of its plausibility, or rather, its truth.

ST. CYRIL – Therefore just as when the flesh of the Word Who gives life to all beings came into being it overcame the power of death and corruption, the same way, I think, His soul is free from all sin and was fixed as a strong immutable condition in all sorts of good, and from old, reigns incomparably stronger over sin. Indeed, Christ is the first Man, He "Who committed no sin, nor was deceit found in His mouth"[96], just as He is the Source (ῥίζα) and First-fruits (απαρχη) for those who are appointed into the "newness of life"[97] in the Spirit, and the incorruption of the body, and the divine stability and security, now He will guide the human race as a participation and a grace to them. Recognizing this, the divine Paul wrote: "And as we have borne the image of the man of dust, we shall also bear the Image of the heavenly Man".[98] By "the unstable image of the man of dust," he means sin and death, that has been launched against us; by "the image of heavenly," that is to say of Christ, the steadfastness in the sanctification and renewal which brings us back from death and corruption to incorruptibility and to life.

---

[96] 1 Pet. 2:22; Is. 53:9.
[97] Rom. 6:4.
[98] 1 Cor. 15:49.

We therefore affirm that the Word was fully united to humanity. For it is impossible that the best part in us, that is to say the soul, would have been made not worthy of anyone's thinking, attributing the sufferings of His coming to the flesh only. The economy of the Mystery, therefore, was accomplished through both. He made use of His own flesh, on the one hand, as an instrument for the works of the flesh and physical weaknesses, and much disgrace, and of His own soul, on the other hand, for the human yet blameless sufferings. For it says that He hungered, and that He was brought under distress from long journeys, as well as terror, fears, grieving, agony, and death upon the Cross. Compelled by no one, He gave up His own soul for us, "that He might be Lord of both the dead and the living".[99] Redeeming all flesh with His own flesh, a gift truly worthy, making [His] soul the redemption of all souls, if it will live again, existing, like God, as life by nature. The divine Peter said, "Men and brethren, let me speak freely to you of the patriarch David, that he is both dead and buried, and his tomb is with us to this day. Therefore, being a prophet, and knowing that God had sworn with an oath to him that of the fruit of his body, according to the flesh, He would raise up the Christ to sit on his throne, he, foreseeing this, spoke concerning the resurrection of the Christ, that His soul was not left in Hades, nor did His flesh see corruption".[100]

---

[99] Rom. 14:9.
[100] Acts 2:29-31.

For it would be unlawful to say of Him that corruption is able to lay hold permanently of the flesh united with the Word or that the Divine soul could be gripped by the gates of Hades. "He was not left in Hades," as the divine Paul said. For he said that, the nature that is entirely unreachable and indestructible by death, that is the Divinity of the Only-Begotten, did not remain in the depths of the earth. He Who is inconceivable fills everything and dwells everywhere by His Divine energy, and miraculous nature. For the quality of Divinity is higher than places, limitations, and measured majesty, He Himself permeated by nothing. The paradox which no one can but wonder at, is that the body will live again, that which is corrupt by nature. For it is united with the incorruptible Word. As for the Divine soul, which obtained from Him a concourse and unification, it had descended into Hades, submitting to the Divine power and authority, appearing to the spirits there. Accordingly, He also declared, "to those in bondage, come out; to those in darkness, be revealed".[101] It seems to me that the Divine Peter said this very thing concerning the Word of God and His soul, which became united to Him by the economy. "For it is better, if it is the will of God, to suffer for doing good than for doing evil. or Christ also suffered once for sins, the just for the unjust, that He might bring us to God, being put to death in the flesh but made alive by the Spirit by whom also He went and preached to the spirits in prison,

---

[101] Is. 49:9.

who formerly were disobedient".[102] I suppose also they would not say that the Divinity of the Only-Begotten descended into Hades unveiled [with humanity], but rather it proclaimed to the spirits there, being altogether hidden. For the Divinity always surpasses sight. But we will not suggest that He assumed the form of the soul itself by appearance and form. Let this opinion be disregarded everywhere! But just as He dwelt with the flesh among those of the flesh, in the same manner He preached to the souls in Hades, Himself carrying His own united soul.

And it is perhaps deeply rooted, truly mysterious, and difficult to grasp for our minds, the manner of the union, so it is fitting to meditate on that. For to be concerned with what is not ours is not without consequences, since it is most foolish to stress over things that are above intelligence, and to try to grasp by the mind what is not possible to grasp. Or do you not know that this profound Mystery, which is above our mind, is honored with faithfulness that is not to be curiously examined? He said unknowingly, "how can these things be?"[103], attributing it to Nicodemus and those like him, while we will undoubtedly accept the things prophesied by the Spirit of God, and we will believe in Christ Himself, saying with Him, "Most assuredly, We speak what

---

[102] 1 Pet. 3:17-19.
[103] John 3:9.

We know, and testify what We have seen".[104]

HERMIAS – Well said.

ST. CYRIL – So, let this total nonsense vanish--this powerless myth, this false opinion, and this imposed trivial matter that is quibbled about. For we do not accept at all the injury of the Begotten, even though those adorned with envy beat us down with such sharp words. For the divine Mystery of ours is "not with persuasive words of human wisdom, but in demonstration of the Spirit".[105]

Therefore, while the Lord and God of all exists from the beginning, according to the Scriptures, the Only-Begotten appeared to us. For He was seen upon the earth, and shone forth to those in darkness (cf. Luke 1:79), becoming man, neither in appearance--God forbid, for it is insanity to think or speak thus--nor introduced into the flesh according to a transformation and conversion, since the Word of God is unchangeable and always possesses what is His, since He Himself is the Maker of the ages. Nor still as though He were an unsubstantial Word, nor becoming a mere utterance in a man, for He is the One Who, calling the things that do not exist, has compelled them into existence and birth, for He is the Life that shone forth from the life of God and Father, and is spiritually

---

[104] John 3:11.
[105] 1 Cor. 2:4.

apprehended according to His own hypostasis. And not that He put on the flesh alone, impoverished of a rational soul, but He was born of a woman in truth, and became man, Who is living, existing, and co-Eternal with God; and the Logos of God the Father, taking the form of a bondservant (cf. Phil. 2:7), just as He remains perfect in divinity, is also perfect in humanity--being not a composite (συγκείμενος) of the divinity only and the flesh into one Christ, Lord and Son, but as I say, out of the two perfections, the humanity and the divinity, bound together paradoxically into one and the same.

HERMIAS – Who, therefore, did the Holy Virgin bear? The man, or the Word of God?

ST. CYRIL – Here indeed is the confusion, and the mistake against the appropriateness and the truth! For, to me, if you separate; or even set apart Emmanuel into man, individually, and the Word of God--then you would refashion our Emmanuel into two persons (διπρόσωπον)! This is what was said by a disciple of Christ: "But you, beloved, remember the words which were spoken before by the apostles of our Lord Jesus Christ: how they told you that there would be mockers in the last time who would walk according to their own ungodly lusts. These are sensual persons, who cause divisions, not having the Spirit".[106]

HERMIAS – Should you not therefore distinguish in any way?

---

[106] Jude 1:17-19.

CHRISTOLOGICAL DIALOGUE

ST. CYRIL – Certainly not. And especially not to speak of two after the union and conceive each of them separately. It is necessary to know, as a result, that the mind contemplates some distinction of natures, for divinity and humanity are certainly not the same thing, but at the same time to admit, concerning these concepts, the both coming together into union. Accordingly, as God He comes forth from God the Father, and from the Virgin, as man. For, the ineffable Word of God that is above all understanding, having shone forth, was engendered, it is said, from a woman, having descended into humanity, and established Himself as though He was not; not to remain emptied, but to be believed to be God, even when He was manifest on earth in a form such as ours, not as though living in a man but Himself became man by nature, while maintaining His glory to Himself. So these two elements so far from any consubstantiality, separated by an immeasurable difference, humanity and divinity, the divine Paul brings them together into one through the economy, thus indicating that both consist of the one Christ, Son and God: "Paul, a bondservant of Jesus Christ, called to be an apostle, separated to the gospel of God which He promised before through His prophets in the Holy Scriptures, concerning His Son Jesus Christ our Lord, who was born of the seed of David according to the flesh, and declared to be the Son of God with power according to the Spirit of holiness".[107] This is

---

[107] Rom. 1:1-4.

clearly stated "separated to the gospel of God," while writing bluntly: "For we do not preach ourselves, but Christ Jesus the Lord"[108]; and again: "For I determined not to know anything among you except Jesus Christ and Him crucified".[109] While calling Him the Son of God, Paul also says that Christ was born of the seed of David and says He was recognized as the Son of God. How then, tell me, is it that God comes from "the seed" of David? The Son before all ages, eternal as the existence of God, how could He be designated Son of God, as if He was actually called into existence? He even said about Himself: "The Lord said: 'You are My Son, today I have begotten You"[110]; and yet the word "today" indicates not the past, but the present!

HERMIAS – This was vexing me greatly, and I dare to say that many others found it was difficult to understand as well.

ST. CYRIL – For those who separate and divide, it is enough to give them trouble and embarrassment, however, for those on the contrary, who preserve the unity in Emmanuel, it is easy to achieve the authentic knowledge of holy dogmas. For, the Son Who is co-eternal with the One Who begat Him before all ages, when He descended into human nature, without loss to [His essence] as God,

---

[108] 2 Cor. 4:5.

[109] 1 Cor. 2:2.

[110] Ps. 2:7.

but by assuming humanity can legitimately be conceived as coming from the seed of David and most recently, having a human birth. For what He assumed was not foreign to Him, but truly His own. Similarly, one can consider the composition of a human being. From dissimilars, his nature is composed, I mean the soul and body; and yet the combination is conceived as a single man. Just as the one flesh sometimes points to the whole being and by naming the soul, we think of it together, is in the same way [is the case] of Christ. Because there is only one Son, and one Lord Jesus Christ, before the flesh and man appeared; and we will not deny the Master Who redeemed us, even if it happens that we indicate His human weaknesses and the levels of His descent.

HERMIAS – I am not doing well, and I would like a clear explanation.

ST. CYRIL – Our Lord Jesus Christ said, speaking to the Jews: "If you were Abraham's children, then you would do the works of Abraham. But now you seek to kill Me, a Man who has told you the truth that I heard from God. Abraham did not do this".[111] Paul wrote: Who, "in the days of His flesh, when He had offered up prayers and supplications, with vehement cries and tears to Him who was able to save Him from death, and was heard because of His godly fear, though He was a Son, yet He learned obedience by the

---

[111] John 8:39-40.

things which He suffered".[112] Shall we consider Christ, therefore, to be a mere man, who had no higher purpose than ours?

HERMIAS – God forbid!

ST. CYRIL – Will we allow the Wisdom and power of God to descend into such weakness so as to fear death, and plead to the Father to save Him? And shall we exclude from Emmanuel His being Life by nature? Or, turning to the humanity, and our meager nature which is poor in reason, will we perform something of the things that are praiseworthy, and out of which, will we perceive that God is His transcendent glory, and understand that He Himself is man and God, in fact, the Incarnate God (Θεον ενηνθρωπηκότα)?

HERMIAS – How so? Tell me.

ST. CYRIL – Let the most respected Paul come in our midst then, shouting thus and saying: "However, we speak wisdom among those who are mature, yet not the wisdom of this age nor of the rulers of this age, who are coming to nothing. But, we speak of the wisdom of God in a mystery, the hidden wisdom which God ordained before the ages for our glory, which none of the rulers of this age knew, for if they had, they would not have crucified the Lord of glory".[113] And again: "Who being the brightness (radiance) of His glory and the express Image of His Person, and upholding all things by the word

---

[112] Heb. 5:7-8.

[113] 1 Cor. 2:6-8.

of His power, when He had by Himself purged our sins, sat down at the right hand of the Majesty on high, having become so much better than the angels, as He has by inheritance obtained a more excellent name than they".[114] In fact, being called "Lord of the glory," How is He not far above and beyond all creatures and submissive beings? And what is the human species: it is very little. Even concerning the angels, I would say the groups of Powers, Thrones and Dominions, we even keep in memory the most superior Seraphim, and we certainly recognize that they remain well below His high splendor – at least if one does not have a corrupted mind. For these privileges are, I affirm, extraordinary and it is necessary to attribute it to the only nature that rules the universe. Therefore, how could the Lord of glory be crucified? The radiance of the Father, the character of His being, the One Who carries everything with the words of His power, is said to have become superior to angels, without doubt, I think, because He assumed what is more superior through His manifestation as a man. He writes: "But we see Jesus, who was made a little lower than the angels, for the suffering of death crowned with glory and honor, that He, by the grace of God, might taste death for everyone".[115] Shall we deprive therefore, the Word begotten of God the Father, from any transcendence rightful to His essence, which is exactly similar to

---

[114] Heb. 1:3-4.

[115] Heb. 2:9.

the Father, even if we see Him lower in glory than the angels because of His inferiority according to the economy?

HERMIAS – Certainly not! Because you should neither deprive, in my opinion, the Word of God from the human weakness after the union with the flesh, nor deprive the divine glory of the human element if we think of it as included in Christ. Some people will ask however: "But Who is Jesus Christ really? The man [born] from the Virgin, or the Word [begotten] from God?

ST. CYRIL – It is frankly a silly thing to prolong pointlessly to answer such foolish nonsense. Let me just say that it is perilous and not harmless to cut into two the man and the Word: the economy does not tolerate it, and the divinely-inspired Scripture proclaims that Christ is One. I say that it is necessary that you neither isolate the Word of God from humanity, nor to say that Jesus Christ, the temple born of a woman is not united to the Word. Because the Word of God, Who is considered the Christ, is united to humanity by an ineffable union. Higher than humanity, as God and Son by nature, He sunk slightly below the glory that is due for a God, as a man. As He said earlier: "He who has seen Me has seen the Father, I and the Father are One"[116], sometimes on the contrary: "My Father is greater than I"--not because He is less than the Father, provided that He is identical in substance, but He said inferior

---

[116] John 14:9.

because He is in humanity. The Holy Scriptures also proclaim Him sometimes fully as a man, remaining silent by the economy of His divinity, sometimes on the other hand as God, silently of His humanity. They do Him no harm there, given the coming together of both elements into union.

HERMIAS – What do you mean? I do not quite understand.

ST. CYRIL – The Hebrew from Hebrews, born from the tribe of Benjamin (cf. Phil. 3:5), the Apostle by calling, writes to those whom the faith justified, who mortified the members of the flesh, or even I want to say fornication and passion, evil desires, the covetousness (cf. Col. 3:5): "For you died, and your life is hidden with Christ in God".[117] Christ Himself said about His disciples: "Holy Father, keep through Your Name those whom You have given Me, that they may be one as We are. While I was with them in the world, I kept them in Your Name, those whom You gave Me I have kept; and none of them is lost except the son of perdition, that the Scripture might be fulfilled. But now I come to You, and these things I speak in the world, that they may have My joy fulfilled in themselves".[118] Listen and realize that He was from the same human nature as ours, it is apparent, as represented in these passages.

---

[117] Col. 3:3.
[118] John 17:11-13.

HERMIAS – You are absolutely right.

ST. CYRIL – Let us not think He is hidden or has left the world, since He clearly states: "For where two or three are gathered together in My name, I am there in the midst of them"[119]; and again: "I am with you always, even to the end of the age".[120] Moreover, you can see Saint Paul personally neglecting often the necessity of announcing Christ as being also a man: "Paul, an apostle not from men nor through man, but through Jesus Christ".[121] And again to them: "But I make known to you, brethren, that the gospel which was preached by me is not according to man. For I neither received it from man, nor was I taught it, but it came through the revelation of Jesus Christ".[122] Elsewhere he says: "Even though we have known Christ according to the flesh, yet now we know Him thus no longer".[123] Who thus is this Jesus Christ Who made this divine revelation so infallible and unspeakable of its intimate mysteries shine in Him? Didn't the Word take flesh and for us He did not disdain to be born from a woman?

HERMIAS – Surely yes. For I will remember the words of the Blessed Gabriel to the Holy Virgin: "Do not be afraid, Mary, and

---

[119] Mt. 18:20.
[120] Mt. 28:20.
[121] Gal. 1:1.
[122] Gal. 1:11-12.
[123] 2 Cor. 5:16.

behold, you will conceive in your womb and bring forth a Son, and shall call His name Jesus".[124] This is a new name, I think, that the Father gives to the Word through the voice of an angel! For thus had declared the prophetic oracle: "You shall be called by a new Name, which the mouth of the Lord will name".[125]

ST. CYRIL – When, therefore, the Only-Begotten Son Who is co-eternal with the Father, and before all ages, became man in the last days being born of a woman, He was also called the Firstborn and surrounded by "many brethren".[126] Then also, His Father by nature chose a Name for Him, using His paternal rights, in order that we might similarly speak, following the laws. For having understood the manner of the economy, you would bring us the greatest joy.

HERMIAS – Consequently, it is the same, both Only Son and First-born.

ST. CYRIL – Do not think, my dear that it is otherwise. He is indeed the Only-Begotten, as God, the first born among us by the union of the economy, and as a man, surrounded by many brethren. In order that we too, in Him and through Him, become natural sons of God through the grace. By nature, in Him and in Him only; by participation and by grace, through Him in the Spirit. Just as the

---

[124] Luke 1:20.
[125] Is. 62:2.
[126] Rom. 8:29.

Only-Begotten assumed humanity in Christ through His union with the Word, according to the reconciliation planned by the economy, in the same way it became the property of the Word to be a First-born surrounded by a multitude of brethren through His union with the flesh. Remaining steadfastly God, always existing above change, He does not depart from His own glory. Accordingly, the holy and all-blessed multitude of the celestial spirits as well as us were urged to worship Him. Of course it was very likely, in fact, that they refuse to worship and become reluctant to honor this humble man, and not to deem worthy of glory the One Who became for us such as we are, pushing furthest away from them even the appearance of error. For the Mystery of Christ was invisible to them too, but the Spirit revealed it to them which did not permit these sanctified beings to blaspheme. Hence these words of the divine Paul: "And again, when He brings in the Firstborn into the world, He says: 'Let all the angels of God worship Him'".[127] Indeed, He Who, by the power of His nature, transcends the whole world existing as God outside of it, is introduced as a man, and appears as a part of the universe though not deprived of the divine glory. Because of this: we worship the Only-Begotten Son and we may call Him the Firstborn as it is appropriate, it is very clear, taking into account the humanity.

HERMIAS – Are we to worship Emmanuel as a man, then?

---

[127] Heb. 1:6.

ST. CYRIL – God forbid! This is nonsense, delusion, an aberration. We are then no different from those who have worshipped a creature other than the Creator and Author, "who exchanged the truth of God for the lie"[128], according to what is written, with whom if we should think we are brothers, we will hear exactly the same verse: "Professing to be wise, they became fools, and changed the glory of the incorruptible God into an image made like corruptible man—and birds and four-footed animals and creeping things".[129] Will we not be equal in deed and thoughts with those who were just mentioned, substituting the glory of God falsely with the likeness of the image of the perishable man, if we offer worship to Emmanuel as a mere man and one of us?

HERMIAS – Yes indeed.

ST. CYRIL – What? Would not the heavenly multitude of angels themselves have been mentioned, arriving at such insanity?

HERMIAS – It will be necessary.

ST. CYRIL – Inevitably, I think, we will also place the verdict of error on a crowd of nations, and the stigma of their ancient accusation will remain indelible. Because they are wrong, it seems now as much as before, they have not managed to find the right path. In vain, it seems, that the blessed Paul addressed them saying:

---

[128] Rom. 1:25.

[129] Rom. 1:22.

"But then, indeed, when you did not know God, you served those which by nature are not gods. But now after you have known God, or rather are known by God, how is it that you turn again to the weak and beggarly elements, to which you desire again to be in bondage?"[130] What kind of God did they know, if Christ in whom they believed was not God by nature? But if they worshipped a man, they are entering into the net of the ancient sin. Or isn't what I say true?

HERMIAS – Yes of course!

ST. CYRIL – You see, then in conclusion, we are compelled towards the reasonable necessity to worship the Son as God by nature, even when He has become manifest in our form, having as sufficient the coming together of both elements in the unity, to remove any suspicion which would bother us regarding His humanity.

HERMIAS – What do you mean?

ST. CYRIL – Since the moment that the nature of the Word assumed the humanity, it is no longer simple humanity. Rather, conquering what He assumed by means of His own glory, the Divine glory being preserved in immovable permanence. That was the understanding the disciples had when they worshiped Him,

---

[130] Gal. 4:8-9.

saying: "Truly, You are the Son of God".[131] Seeing Him walking on foot in the flesh like us, He miraculously ran on the crest of waves, as God.

HERMIAS – And who also said to the Samaritan woman: "You worship what you do not know; We know what we worship".[132] Thus, how is one who is counted among the worshipers be worshipped?

ST. CYRIL – At first, my dear, you always cry out this word: "who" an expression invented, I do not know how, by the ignorant. For Christ is not divided at all. The One Who spoke to this poor woman was only the Lord Jesus Christ, consisting mysteriously of the worshipping humanity and of the worshipped divinity, as far as we could again say in a different way concerning Him. For He is simply God, we can conceive Him as the Lord of glory; as far as He became a man Begotten of God in His glory by participation, He asked for this glory by saying: "Father, glorify Your Son"[133], but, "There is one Lord, one faith, one baptism"[134], as it is written. Therefore, just as there is one faith in Christ; and truly in one baptism, as we are baptized, and have believed in the Father, and the Son, and the Holy Spirit; in the same way, and for the same reason, one is our worship

---

[131] Mt. 14:33.
[132] John 4:22.
[133] John 17:5.
[134] Eph. 4:5.

of the Father, the Incarnate Son, and the Holy Spirit. For it is necessary that we shall not at all omit the worship of the Only-Begotten Son, He will be excluded by no means from the worship which is due to Him from our part and from that of the holy angels even though He was incarnate, lived among us, and was called the First-born among many brethren. Since the word of faith concerning Him became something, is it not worth consideration? They would not say, I suppose, those who should choose to think correctly that we believed that He is only the Word of God stripping Him of the flesh. In contrast, this is what we will not pass to say without having said.

HERMIAS – What is the saying?

ST. CYRIL – The faith is not as in one of us, nor in a man, but in God by nature and truly in the face (προσώπω) of Christ. In support of this, here is what the wise Paul writes, "For we do not preach ourselves, but Jesus Christ as Lord, and ourselves as your servants for Jesus' sake. For it is the God Who commanded light to shine out of darkness, Who has shone in our hearts to give us the light of the knowledge of the glory of God in the face of Christ".[135] Behold, the radiance of the knowledge of God the Father has shown in the face of Christ clearly and visibly. Also He said: "He who has seen

---

[135] 2 Cor. 4:6.

CHRISTOLOGICAL DIALOGUE

Me has seen the Father. I and the Father are One".[136]

But the divine character is not material; it is in the power and glory most befitting to God. This is unmixed (ακραιφνές) in Christ. He also deemed it worthy that He be known through it, and He wished to raise up His listeners to contemplating through the superiority of His actions. In spite of His condescension into the visible flesh. "If I do not do the works of My Father, do not believe Me; but if I do them, though you do not believe Me, believe the works".[137] In my opinion, Christ spoke so at this moment not ignorant of the benefit these words will have. Some supposed that He is not God by nature, the One Who became man like us, and taking Him simply as a man similar to us, they made the faith intolerant of Him. So cutting short, in a binding way, their fears and their laziness, He directs the faith to His divine nature, as in the face of the Father. Attributing nothing to the baseness which is like ours, He said: "He who believes in Me, believes not in Me but in Him Who sent Me. And he who sees Me sees Him Who sent Me".[138] It is not equivalent to say: O you who obey My words, do not form a small and low opinion of Me; know instead that by putting your faith in Me Whom you see in the flesh you will not have believed simply in a man, but in the Very Father through Me, I

---

[136] John 14:9, 10:30.
[137] John 10:37-38.
[138] John 12:44-45.

Who am equal to Him in everything, being the immutable Son, Who took flesh for you, and put on this humble garment (περίβλημα), the humanity, though I am equal with Him in nature and in work, and altogether having the same undiminished glory with Him?

HERMIAS – This is true.

ST. CYRIL – You should learn another issue, not tearing asunder the Faith, but admitting no divisions or distinctions in it, regarding His true character, even if He had become flesh. Indeed, when He healed the blind and put him in the sweetness of the light, he marveled from it all, as expected. But he who was cured from suffering was questioned by the Jews and he acknowledged the healer, and meeting him, Christ asked: "'Do you believe in the Son of God?' He answered and said, 'Who is He, Lord that I may believe in Him?' And Jesus said to him, 'You have both seen Him and it is He Who is talking with you.' Then he said, 'Lord, I believe!' And he worshiped Him".[139] Yet how is it not obvious to everyone that the supreme and divine nature is perfectly invisible – "No one has seen God at any time"[140], as it is written. Consequently, if the Word of God the Father had separated from Himself humanity as [simply] having appeared [as man], and deemed it worthy to believe in Him

---

[139] John 9:35-38.
[140] 1 John 4:12.

only and without the flesh, would He not rather have ordered the cured person to discover by reasoning God's nature and what kind of manner it is, rather than showing it in a physical reality, as if eyes could perceive him: "You have both seen Him and it is He Who is talking with you." Or shall we say that He did not exhibit His own flesh?

HERMIAS – Certainly not.

ST. CYRIL – So how could the flesh be Him, if we were to understand this not in terms of the union, as He Himself belonging to what is His own, as though He could become lazy as we are? It would give an implication that the man like us is neither divided nor imperfect, who is composed of soul and a body, not to be designated only by flesh.

HERMIAS – Sure, what you say is right.

ST. CYRIL – The wise John has also written somewhere: "Jesus did many other miraculous signs in the presence of His disciples, which are not written in this book; but these are written that you may believe that Jesus is the Christ, the Son of God, and that believing you may have life in His Name".[141] It is not any different than that which we hear the divine Peter, addressing the Jews, clearly and publicly saying: "Rulers of the people and elders of Israel: If we this day are judged for a good deed done to a helpless man, by what

---

[141] John 20:30-31.

means he has been made well, let it be known to you all, and to all the people of Israel, that by the Name of Jesus Christ of Nazareth, Whom you crucified, Whom God raised from the dead, by Him this man stands here before you whole".[142] And further: "Nor is there salvation in any other, for there is no other Name under heaven given among men by which we must be saved".[143] And Who is He who suffers death, Who was resurrected in glory, Who is from Nazareth, except Jesus Christ, Who before all ages was begotten ineffably of God the Father and born bodily from a woman at the fullness of time? Whoever embraces faith in Christ will receive a distinguished privilege. He will be called the son of God. "But as many as received Him, to them He gave the right to become children of God, to those who believe in His name: who were born, not of blood, nor of the will of the flesh, nor of the will of man, but of God".[144] For "that in all things He may have the preeminence"[145], as it is written, He was born of a woman. And because it is the restoration of a distorted creation, brought back to God through sanctification, it is manifest before all the other acts of the Spirit. He surpassed all intimacy between a man and a woman, not to incriminate the act as shameful or dishonorable – marriage is

---

[142] Acts 4:8-10.
[143] Acts 4:12.
[144] John 1:12-13.
[145] Col. 1:18.

something honorable, and the Creator in the beginning made them male and female – but now He led humanity to something greater and incomparably higher, He wanted us to be born of the Spirit, not of men. So He said: "Do not call anyone on earth your father; for One is your Father, He Who is in heaven, and you are all brethren".[146] Therefore, it incurs absolutely no reproach to believe in Him, it is rewarded by the forgiveness of sins. Here indeed the elected Paul writes: "knowing that a man is not justified by the works of the law but by faith in Jesus Christ, even we have believed in Christ Jesus, that we might be justified by faith in Christ and not by the works of the law".[147] Now I do not hesitate to come back to what I said earlier, for we do not hear that the Word of God existed in Himself, but He added the human element and was born in the flesh. It is when we saw Him in that condition when He happened to be in a form such as ours, that the Father spoke to the Apostles, in a voice from heaven saying: "This is My Beloved Son, in Whom I am well pleased: hear Him".[148] Notice that He does not say, "In Him is My Son," so let them not conceive a being enclosed in another, but One and the Same, by virtue of union desired by the economy. That this is a very dangerous conclusion, John convinces us by writing: "He who believes in the Son of God has the witness

---

[146] Mt. 23:9, 8.

[147] Gal. 2:16.

[148] Mt. 17:5.

in himself; he who does not believe God has made Him a liar, because he has not believed the testimony that God has given of His Son".[149] This is His testimony: He, along with His flesh, in the form of a slave, is strictly my undivided and true Son. But who? Received the glorious grace of the holy baptism, coming to life in Him, participating in sanctification of God in the Spirit, all that shall grant us that it is the work of Jesus Christ?

HERMIAS – Indeed I remember what John says: "I indeed baptize you with water unto repentance, but He who is coming after me is mightier than I, whose sandals I am not worthy to carry. He will baptize you with the Holy Spirit and fire".[150]

ST. CYRIL – Shall we then, my friend, say that this is the work of humanity such as ours that was able to baptize in the Holy Spirit and fire?

HERMIAS – How could this be?

ST. CYRIL – And indeed, talking about a man who is not present nor yet seen, John says that He baptizes with fire and the Holy Spirit, not in the manner of a slave or in the manner of a servant instilling a Spirit that is not His, but as a God by nature with authority from above, which is of Him and belongs to Him, through which the Divine character is engraved in us. Indeed we are formed

---

[149] 1 John 5:9-10.
[150] Mt. 3:11.

anew in the divine image in Christ Jesus, not that we felt a new shaping of our bodies – it would be really easy to imagine just that – but through partaking (μεταλαχεῖν) of the Holy Spirit, possessing Christ Himself in us, to the point that our joy is to shout: "I will greatly rejoice in the Lord, My soul shall be joyful in my God; For He has clothed me with the garments of salvation, He has covered me with the robe of righteousness".[151] "For," he said, "as many of you as were baptized into Christ have put on Christ".[152]

HERMIAS – It is therefore in a man that we were baptized? Shall we say that this is the truth?

ST. CYRIL – Silence, man! What are you doing? You are flattening our hopes to the ground. For we have not been baptized in a mere man, but in the Incarnate God Who forgives past sins to all those who have accepted faith in Him. This is what the divine Peter said when he addressed the Jews, saying: "Repent, and let every one of you be baptized in the Name of Jesus Christ for the remission of sins; and you shall receive the gift of the Holy Spirit".[153] For He forgives sins to the one devoted to Him, and anoints the rest of us with His own Spirit, as He Himself instills Him in us as the Word of God the Father, and makes us rise above the nature that is in us, and places something shared with the economy of the flesh, because

---

[151] Is. 61:10.
[152] Gal. 3:27.
[153] Acts 2:38.

of the union, and as a man He breathes in the flesh. He breathed into His Apostles saying: "Receive the Holy Spirit".[154] In the words of John, "God does not give the Spirit by measure"[155], but He Himself sends Him out of Himself, just as the Father. We also see the divine Paul, without any difference on this point, attributing that Spirit to God the Father and to the Son. Here indeed is what he wrote: "But you are not in the flesh but in the Spirit, if indeed the Spirit of God dwells in you. Now if anyone does not have the Spirit of Christ, he is not His. And if Christ is in you, the body is dead because of sin, but the Spirit is life because of righteousness".[156]

HERMIAS – This is agreeable: the Spirit of the Son. Not only as the Son Who is the Word begotten of the Father, but even if He has become a man like us.

ST. CYRIL – He is the Word begotten of and consubstantial with the Father -even if it is said that He received the Spirit when He became a man – which by nature, deprives Him of the properties of divinity. Also, since He Himself is the life of all beings, because of His ineffable birth from the living Father, He is said to be the Giver of Life among us. It is then similarly possible to see Him on the one

---

[154] John 20:22.
[155] John 3:34.
[156] Rom. 8:9-10.

hand given the glory of His Divine energy to His flesh, while on the other hand that He assimilated the things of the flesh and in some way, as if by means of the economic union, they are attributed it to His own nature.

HERMIAS – How so? Who speaks thus?

ST. CYRIL – Would you not rather say that it is appropriate for the Word of God the Father by nature to have come down from heaven, and that He is able to give life to all beings to whom He wished to instill life?

HERMIAS – Yes, I would say that.

ST. CYRIL – What? And the divine power to create, tell me, would you grant that it belongs to humanity?

HERMIAS – Me? Not at all!

ST. CYRIL – How then does He give us life as God, except not only through partaking of the Holy Spirit, but also by offering the flesh He assumed as food? For He said, "Most assuredly, I say to you, unless you eat the flesh of the Son of Man and drink His blood, you have no life in you".[157] While the Jews were vehemently attacking Him, and throwing stones at those who are more noble, I do not know how, having similarly set against the Blessed Moses, they cried out loud, "Our fathers ate the manna in the desert; as it is

---

[157] John 6:53.

written, 'He gave them bread from heaven to eat,' What sign will You perform then, that we may believe You?.[158] What will You do, if Your Body really came from the sky above to us?" He said, "Most assuredly, I say to you, Moses did not give you the bread from heaven, but My Father gives you the true bread from heaven. For the bread of God is He Who comes down from heaven and gives life to the world".[159] And again to them, almost pointing with His finger at Himself in the flesh, "I am the living bread which came down from heaven. If anyone eats of this bread, he will live forever; and the bread that I shall give is My flesh, which I shall give for the life of the world. He who eats My flesh and drinks My blood abides in Me, and I in him. As the living Father sent Me, and I live because of the Father, so he who feeds on Me will live because of Me".[160] Furthermore, how is it not precise to say that the flesh has not descended from heaven, but came from the Virgin, according to the Scriptures? The Word is not eaten, but gathering the two into one, and uniting the properties of both natures with one another, as is apparent to us through a thousand words. For Nicodemus, not understanding the Mystery, cried out ignorantly, "How can these things be?"[161], and He said, "If I have told you earthly things and

---

[158] John 6:31-30.

[159] John 6:32-33.

[160] John 6:51, 56-57.

[161] John 3:9.

you do not believe, how will you believe if I tell you heavenly things? No one has ascended to heaven but He Who came down from heaven, that is, the Son of Man Who is in heaven".[162] And to the Jews being sick like Nicodemus with equal stupidity, and choosing to mock Him, I do not know how, because He said that His body gives life and is from heaven. "Does this offend you? What then if you should see the Son of Man ascend where He was before?"[163] Or will we not say that Emmanuel was born of a woman?

HERMIAS – How to deny it?

ST. CYRIL – So where was He before? Or how did He go up there as He Himself said He did, when His united body was born of the Holy Virgin? Do we refuse to admit also that the flesh from the earth is, in terms of its nature, powerless to give life?

HERMIAS – It is true.

ST. CYRIL – How, then, tell me, the flesh gives life? Or how should that which is from the earth be thought of as coming from heaven?

HERMIAS – I think according to the union of the living Word that is from heaven.

ST. CYRIL – That is thinking quite rightly and in accordance with

---

[162] John 3:12-13.
[163] John 6:61-62.

the sacred writings. Otherwise there would be no divine Creator and He would be no longer thought of separate from His flesh. To guarantee what I say, I will once more quote the divine Paul writing here that: "giving thanks to the Father Who has qualified us to be partakers of the inheritance of the saints in the light. He has delivered us from the power of darkness and conveyed us into the kingdom of the Son of His love, in whom we have redemption through His blood, the forgiveness of sins. He is the Image of the invisible God, the Firstborn over all creation. For by Him all things were created that are in heaven and that are on earth, visible and invisible, whether Thrones or Dominions or Principalities or Powers. All things were created through Him and for Him. And He is before all things, and in Him all things consist. And He is the Head of the body, the Church, Who is the beginning, the Firstborn from the dead, that in all things He may have the preeminence. For it pleased the Father that in Him all the fullness should dwell, and by Him to reconcile all things to Himself, by Him, whether things on earth or things in heaven".[164] Behold again Paul openly declares that all things were created through Him and unto Him, and He is before all things and in Him are all things, and he says He is the Firstborn from the dead, Who has made peace through His blood between those of the heavens and those of the earth. Therefore, Who is the Firstborn from the dead, but Christ Jesus, that is to say

---

[164] Col. 1:12–20.

the Word in flesh and with flesh? For the Word being God, could not die, of course, nor can we regard the Creator of the universe as being a man like us, if He did not create as a God – and if He is not thought of as separate from the flesh after the union. But He is also the Firstborn from the dead, insofar as He appeared as a man, without rejecting His divinity because of the Incarnation. You see in all this something to criticize?

HERMIAS – Not in any way whatsoever!

ST. CYRIL – Elsewhere you would find the inspired writers coming through the same discourse. John for example: "In the beginning was the Word, and the Word was with God, and the Word was God. He was in the beginning with God. All things were made through Him, and without Him nothing was made that was made".[165] And Paul said: "there is one God, the Father, of Whom are all things; and one Lord Jesus Christ, through Whom are all things".[166] However, if after the union of the Word with the flesh, there was some separation (μεσολαβουν), division into two sons, I say, how, in your opinion, have all things been created by Jesus Christ? Now everything has been created by Him. It is therefore evident that the natural properties inherent in the Word from the Father have been preserved even when He became flesh. It is

---

[165] John 1:1–3.
[166] 1 Cor. 8:6.

therefore reckless to dare [to introduce] a severing. For one is the Lord Jesus Christ and through Him the Father created everything.

HERMIAS – True.

ST. CYRIL – So He is the Divine Creator, the Giver of Life, as the Life, composed of both human and super human properties into One Who is in the midst (εν τι το μεταξυ). He is indeed "Mediator between God and men,"[167] according to the Scriptures, God by nature and not separate from the flesh, truly a man, but not as a mere man like us, on the contrary, being just as He was even when He became flesh. For it is written: "Jesus Christ is the same yesterday, today, and forever".[168] Do we not believe in fact that Emmanuel has been born of the Virgin in the fullness of time?

HERMIAS – Yes, for we will not contradict the Scriptures.

ST. CYRIL – Now tell me dear friend, the words "yesterday" and "today" don't they tell us one is in the present time, and one that is already passed?

HERMIAS – Yes.

ST. CYRIL – How, therefore, would He be the same in the past when He has not yet been born in the flesh?

HERMIAS – Because He is the Word from the beginning, and

---

[167] 1 Tim. 2:5.
[168] Heb. 13:8.

having been made manifest from a Father who is eternal and immutable, He also has, by His very nature, eternity and immutability.

ST. CYRIL – All my compliments for this idea. Yes it is true, it is perfectly fair. So please answer my question, my friend, for I am fond of inquiry.

HERMIAS – What question?

ST. CYRIL – Was it not just recently, at the time of the Incarnation, that this Name has been given to the Word: Jesus Christ?

HERMIAS – Well, yes, we have already demonstrated at length.

ST. CYRIL – So you realize: Jesus Christ and not only that the Word is truly the same yesterday, today and forever. But how would that human nature possess the immutability and permanence when it is subjected to change especially a change that makes it go from nothingness to being and to life?

HERMIAS – The truth has left the Sacred Scripture? It says that what did not exist yesterday has pre-existed?

ST. CYRIL – I would never say that, far from it! Yesterday, today and forever Jesus Christ is the same. I will not deny the antiquity (πρεσβύτατον) of the Word, and His immutability in the least degree, even if He became flesh. I think however that He made it clear to us that, according to the union with His own flesh, He exists "yesterday" and is pre-existing. In fact, the deranged Jews loathed Him, and in their rejection of faith undertook to stone Him. They were surprised, in fact, that though He is only a visible man like us, that His own super-human ever-existence, saying: "Most assuredly, I say to you, before Abraham was, I AM".[169] They repeat: "You are not yet fifty years old, and You have seen Abraham!".[170] And John said: "He Who comes after me is preferred before me, for He was before me".[171] Yet how, knowing that Emmanuel is a man and giving Him the name, can He declare that He is born later than him, after him?

HERMIAS – He says that He is before him and born first, according to the glory, at least this is the way I hear it.

ST. CYRIL – I will not need many words to make you understand the delusion, and ignorance of such an idea. For having accepted being before as better in glory, by the same reasoning, we will say, it is very clear that being after means to be second in honor. It apparently follows that, against all common sense, we suppose foolishly that Christ is inferior in glory than John and coming after

---

[169] John 8:58.
[170] John 8:57.
[171] John 1:15.

Him. John says: "After me comes a Man".[172]

HERMIAS – This is nonsense! We believe that this cannot be! If we perceive the true meaning of these words from Psalms: "For who in the heavens can be compared to the Lord? Who among the sons of the mighty can be likened to the Lord?"[173]

ST. CYRIL – Therefore, one must assign ever-existence to Him with His flesh, as God in nature united with flesh, and equally gave the good things of His nature to His own body.

HERMIAS – You speak wonderfully.

ST. CYRIL – Even if these assertions are correct, you can, my friend, realize it, if you want it, from other evidence. For God spoke somewhere through one of the holy prophets concerning the flesh of Christ who is from the seed of David. "But you, Bethlehem Ephrata, though you are little among the thousands of Judah, Yet out of you shall come forth to Me the One to be Ruler in Israel, Whose goings forth are from of old, from everlasting".[174] And the most venerable Paul said this concerning the sons of Israel, "all were baptized into Moses in the cloud and in the sea, all ate the same spiritual food, and all drank the same spiritual drink. For they drank of that spiritual Rock that followed them, and that Rock was

---

[172] John 1:30.
[173] Ps. 89:7.
[174] Micah 5:2.

Christ".[175] Gaze then on Christ Jesus, Who Himself is the most ancient Word according to the economic union. Or is the Word not clear? For He said He is a Man from Bethlehem, and that He has His birth from the beginning of the ages from a woman. For He was from the beginning, and is the Incarnate Word before all ages, and He Himself is the Rock, who gave thirsty Israel to drink from the streams of hope, when He was born in the flesh and humanity in the fullness of time, and was anointed by God the Father for His mission in the world. It was not for another reason that He was called Christ, and the Rock was Christ, according to Paul. Or will you say that, something is questionable?

HERMIAS – Not at all!

ST. CYRIL – In this connection the wise John will also support and strive with us, almost gathering the natures and leading each of the unique properties of the powers to unity. Consider what he says in effect: "What was in the beginning, what we have heard, what we have seen with our eyes, what we beheld and our hands touch the word of life – for Life is manifested, and we have seen, and we bear witness, and we proclaim the eternal life which was with the Father and was manifested to us".[176] Behold he says He saw clearly Him who was from the beginning, and experienced Him and touched

---

[175] 1 Cor. 10:2-4.
[176] 1 John 1:1-2.

CHRISTOLOGICAL DIALOGUE

Him. In fact, Thomas exclaimed: "My Lord and my God"[177], after placing the finger at the side of the body and the holes made by nails. The divine Luke also tells us that the holy Apostles were eyewitnesses and servants of the Word. For the incorporeal became manifest, and the intangible became tangible. For the garment of flesh became no longer foreign, but He made it a temple, and became known with it as God and Lord. You know it, since it has been written by the most venerable Paul, "For none of us lives to himself, and no one dies to himself. For if we live, we live to the Lord; and if we die, we die to the Lord. Therefore, whether we live or die, we are the Lord's. For to this end Christ died and rose and lived again, that He might be Lord of both the dead and the living".[178] Is it well established that He is Lord over the dead and the living, Who had died, and rose for no other reason than that this only?

HERMIAS – Yes, it is established.

ST. CYRIL – And Who therefore, my dear, do we say who suffered death and came back to life?

HERMIAS – The Son of course.

ST. CYRIL – Yes the Son, well said. I compliment you. But I want to learn from you whether the Word of God the Father is mortal

---

[177] John 20:28.
[178] Rom. 14:7-9.

and subject to corruption, or higher above death and corruption, as He is Life?

HERMIAS – I like the second option.

ST. CYRIL – So, how has He become "Free among the dead" according to the Scriptures?[179] The Word Himself could not possibly have died.

HERMIAS – That is it, His flesh is dead, He Himself is said to have suffered death.

ST. CYRIL – That's right, perfectly! Therefore, He is not without flesh, but rather in it and with it He has girded the glory of Lordship, Who died under the law of our flesh and by a similar nature as ours, and rose again. Showing us that the suffering of death is human, while it is Divine activity to rise, so that through both He might be known, both like us and superior to us as God and Lord of all, and after existing with us, He is seen with the Father. Recognizing this, Nathaniel proclaimed: "Rabbi, You are the Son of God! You are the King of Israel!"[180] He Himself told His disciples: "You call me Lord and Master, and you do well, for so I AM".[181] And believing in the work of forgiving sins, He gave power over unclean spirits to cast them out and to cure every disease and

---

[179] Ps. 87:5.
[180] John 1:49.
[181] John 13:13.

every infirmity among the people. Was it not "in the Name of Jesus Christ of Nazareth" (Acts 3:6) that healed the lame man sitting at the gate? He shook off his long-term disability, and thus he escaped the inescapable disease, to whom the divine Paul said, "Aeneas, Jesus Christ heals you".[182]

HERMIAS – True.

ST. CYRIL – So in every way, being oriented towards the truth and eager to follow in the opinion of the Holy Scriptures, and following those of the Fathers, we believe in the One Who comes from the root of Jesse[183]; Who is the seed of David[184]; Who is born of a woman in the flesh; Who, as a man like us was under the law[185], but as God is above us, over and above the law; Who for us and with us was among the dead; Who, above us, is Himself Life-giving and Life. Again, we believe He is truly the Son of God, neither stripping away the human element by the Divinity, nor undressing the Word of His humanity after the ineffable union, but confessing One and the Same Son Who from two realities was ineffably made manifest as One out of both according to the clear union from above, of course, not under a change of nature.

The benefit that will be accrued to those who think this

---

[182] Acts 9:34.
[183] Is. 11:10, Rom. 15:12.
[184] John 7:42; Rom 1:3; 2 Tim. 2:8.
[185] Gal. 4:4.

way, the disciple of Christ makes it known by saying: "Whoever confesses that Jesus Christ is the Son of God, God abides in him and he in God"[186], the wise John testifies that Jesus Christ, who comes from David according to the flesh, is by nature and truly Son of God, according to the Word became flesh and dwelt among us, saying: "And we know that the Son of God is come, and has given us an understanding, that we may know Him Who is true; and we are in Him Who is true, in His Son Jesus Christ. This is the true God, and eternal life"[187], and by Him and with Him, glory is due to God the Father with the Holy Spirit now and ever and to the ages of ages.

Amen.

---

[186] 1 John 4:15.
[187] 1 John 5:20.

Bibliography

Biblioteca medicea laurenziana, and Angelo Maria Bandini. Catalogus codicum manuscriptorum Bibliothecae Mediceae Laurentianae varia continens opera Graecorum Patrum. Florence: Typis Caesareis, 1764.

Campenhausen, Hans Von. The Fathers of the Church. Hendrickson Publishers, Incorporated, 1998.

Cayré, Fulbert. Manual of Patrology and History of Theology: Transl. by H. Howitt. Paris: Desclée, 1935.

Christou, Panagiotis C. Greek patrology II: the literature of the Period of Persecutions. Thessaloniki: Patriarchal Institute for Patristic Studies, 1978.

Cyril, and George Dion Dragas. Against Those Who Are Unwilling to Confess That the Holy Virgin Is Theotokos. Rollinsford, NH: Orthodox Research Institute, 2004.

Cyril, and Georges-Matthieu de Durand. Deux dialogues christologiques. Paris: Du Cerf, 1964.

Cyrille. Deux dialogues christologiques. Paris: Éd. du Cerf, 1964.

Dorner, I. A, and William Lindsay Alexander. History of the Development of the Doctrine of the Person of Christ. Edinburgh: T. & T. Clark, 1868.

Eustratiades, Sophronios, and Arkadios. Catalogue of the Greek Manuscripts in the Library of the Monastery of Vatopedi on Mt.

Athos. Cambridge: Harvard University Press [u.a.], 1924.

Grillmeier, Aloys. Christ in Christian Tradition. Westminster John Knox Press, 1996.

Hardt, Ignaz, Johann Christoph von Aretin, and Königliche Hof- und Staatsbibliothek (München). Catalogus Codicum Manuscriptorum Graecorum Bibliothecae Regiae Bavaricae 1. Monachii, 1806.

Kerrigan, Alexander. St. Cyril of Alexandria, Interpreter of the Old Testament. Roma: Pontificio Istituto Biblico, 1952.

Loon, Hans van. The Dyophysite Christology of Cyril of Alexandria. Leiden; Boston: Brill, 2009. http://public.eblib.com/EBLPublic/PublicView.do?ptiID=489511.

Müntz, Eugène. La Bibliothèque du Vatican au XVe siècle d'après des documents inédits; contributions pour servir à l'histoire de l'humanisme. Paris: E. Thorin, 1887.

Prestige, George Leonard. Fathers and Heretics: Six Studies in Dogmatic Faith with Prologue and Epilogue. London; New York: Society for Promoting Christian Knowledge; Macmillan, 1940.

Quasten, Johannes, and Italy) Istituto patristico Augustinianum (Rome. Patrology. Westminster, Md.: Christian Classics, 1986.

Schaff, Philip. NPNF2-04. Athanasius: Select Works and Letters. CCEL, n.d.

Witherington, Ben. The Problem with Evangelical Theology: Testing the Exegetical Foundations of Calvinism, Dispensationalism, and Wesleyanism. Waco (Tex.): Baylor University press, 2005.

Young, Frances M. From Nicaea to Chalcedon: a Guide to the Literature and Its Background. Philadelphia: Fortress Press, 1983.

Zachariades, G. E. "Saint Cyril of Alexandria by Chrysostom Papadopoulos. Alexandria: Patriarchal Press, 1933. 483 Pages. Drachmae 25." Church History: Studies in Christianity and Culture 3, no. 02 (1934): 168–169. doi:10.1017/S0009640700120876.

Biblical Citations

Exodus

Ex. 3:14   32

Psalms

Ps. 101:26-28   26

Ps. 139:4   28

Ps. 2:7   42

Ps. 5:10   28

Ps. 74:6   29

Ps. 87:5   63

Ps. 89:7   61

Ps. 9:28   28

Proverbs

Prov. 9:18   19

Isaiah

Is. 11:10   64

Is. 49:9   39

Is. 53:9   37

Is. 55:8-9   34

Is. 61:10   55

Is. 62:2   46

Is. 7:14	27

Baruch

Baruch 3:33	25

Micah

Micah 5:2	62

Matthew

Mt. 11:27	21
Mt. 12:24	18
Mt. 14:33	49
Mt. 17:5	53
Mt. 18:20	46
Mt. 23:9, 8	53
Mt. 28:19	22
Mt. 28:20	46
Mt. 3:11	54

Luke

Luke 1:20	46
Luke 1:30–31	21, 27
Luke 2:11-12	22
Luke 2:14	22

John

John 1:12-13	53

CHRISTOLOGICAL DIALOGUE

John 1:1-3	28, 59
John 1:15	61
John 1:30	61
John 1:49	64
John 10:30	50
John 10:37-38	51
John 10:38	31
John 12:44-45	51
John 13:13	64
John 17:11-13	46
John 17:5	49
John 19:34	23
John 20:22	55
John 20:28	62
John 20:30-31	52
John 3:11	39
John 3:12-13	57
John 3:34	55
John 3:9	39, 57
John 4:22	49
John 56-57	57
John 6:31-30	56
John 6:32-33	57
John 6	57
John 6:53	56
John 6:61-62	57
John 7:42	64

John 8:39-40	43
John 8:57	28, 61
John 8:58	61
John 9:35-38	51
John 14:6	32
John 14:8	30
John 14:9	31, 45, 50

Acts

Acts 2:29-31	38
Acts 2:38	55
Acts 4:12	52
Acts 4:8-10	52
Acts 9:34	64

Romans

Rom 1:3	64
Rom. 1:1-4	42
Rom. 1:22	48
Rom. 1:25	48
Rom. 14:9	38, 63
Rom. 15:12	64
Rom. 6:4	37
Rom. 8:29	33, 47
Rom. 8:3-4	35, 36
Rom. 8:9-10	55
Rom. 12:3	33

1 Corinthians

1 Cor. 2:2	42
1 Cor. 2:4	40
1 Cor. 2:6-8	44
1 Cor. 4:7	26
1 Cor. 8:6	59
1 Cor. 10:2-4	62
1 Cor. 12:3	18
1 Cor. 15:12-15	24
1 Cor. 15:14	23
1 Cor. 15:18	23
1 Cor. 15:3-7	23
1 Cor. 15:49	37

2 Corinthians

2 Cor. 4:5	42
2 Cor. 4:6	50
2 Cor. 5:16	46

Galatians

Gal. 1:1	46
Gal. 1:11-12	46
Gal. 2:16	53
Gal. 3:27	55
Gal. 4:4	24, 64

Gal. 4:8-9   48

Ephesians
Eph. 4:5   50

Colossians
Col. 1:12–20   58
Col. 1:18   53
Col. 3:3   45

1 Timothy
1 Tim 2:5   33
1 Tim. 1:7   19
1 Tim. 2:5   59
1 Tim. 3:16   2, 22

2 Timothy
2 Tim. 2:8   64

Philemon
Phil. 1:19   18
Phil. 2:7   24

Hebrews
Heb. 1:3-4   44
Heb. 1:6   47
Heb. 13:8   59

CHRISTOLOGICAL DIALOGUE

Heb. 2:14-15	24, 35, 36
Heb. 2:16	22, 27
Heb. 2:18	23
Heb. 2:9	44
Heb. 4:12	32
Heb. 5:7-8	43

1 Peter

1 Pet. 2:22	37
1 Pet. 3:17-19	39

1 John

1 John 1:1-2	28, 62
1 John 2:22-23	29
1 John 4:12	52
1 John 4:1-3	24
1 John 4:15	64
1 John 5:20	65
1 John 5:9-10	54

Jude

Jude 1:17-19	41

ABOUT THE TRANSLATOR

Emmanuel Gergis is a full deacon in the Coptic Orthodox Church. He is the Co-founder and President of Agora University. He holds a Master of Arts degree in Applied Orthodox Theology from the University of Balamand, and a Master of Letters degree from the University of St. Andrews in Scotland with a focus on Theological Anthropology. Emmanuel completed his doctorate in Systematic and Historical theology from the University of Aberdeen in Scotland where he focused on Coptic epistemology, the unitary reality of Christ, and the theology of T. F. Torrance. He is an author, translator and lecturer on contemporary topics including Orthodox systematic theology, theological anthropology, Trinitarian theology, theological realism, the Alexandrian Patristic tradition, theological epistemology and Coptic Christianity.

Other Titles by the Author:

- *Theological Anthropology Redefined*

AGORA
UNIVERSITY
PRESS

www.ingramcontent.com/pod-product-compliance
Lightning Source LLC
Chambersburg PA
CBHW030529080526
44586CB00011B/369